Adventurous Experiences

Cecelia Frances Page

iUniverse, Inc.
New York   Bloomington

Adventurous Experiences

iUniverse books may be ordered through booksellers or by contacting:

iUniverse
1663 Liberty Drive
Bloomington, IN 47403
www.iuniverse.com
1-800-Authors (1-800-288-4677)

Because of the dynamic nature of the Internet, any Web addresses or links contained in this book may have changed since publication and may no longer be valid. The views expressed in this work are solely those of the author and do not necessarily reflect the views of the publisher, and the publisher hereby disclaims any responsibility for them.

ISBN: 978-1-4401-2870-7 (pbk)
ISBN: 978-1-4401-2871-4 (ebk)

Printed in the United States of America

iUniverse rev. date: 3/19/09

Contents

PREFACE

ADVENTUROUS EXPERIENCES is an exciting, dynamic, nonfiction book of sixty-three short stories and articles about a variety of stimulating topics. Adventure, short stories include Steve Omar, a World Traveler, Adventures at the Great Lakes, Roving Around, African Adventures, Florida Vacationland, Staying in a Barn, Life in Halcyon, Greyhound Bus Journeys, Train Experiences, Marco Polo's Remarkable Experiences.

Travel experiences include The Mediterranean Sea, Australian Fascinations, Life in Germany, Japan Today, New Zealand Enchantment and Fascinating Sea Coasts. Historical topics are Ancient Cities in the World, Antia, an Underwater City, Living in the 16th through the 21st Century and 2012 A.D.

Nature topics are Horrendous Hurricanes, Cactus and Rock Gardens, Fossils and Hollow Trees. Human interest topics are Scammer Tragedies, Awareness Group, Discussions, Roles of Mayors, Worthwhile Ambitions, Attractive Hairstyles, Facing Obstacles, Abuses and Mistreatment, Maurine's Challenge, Victories, Amazon Women and Anastasia from the Siberian Taiga.

Miscellaneous topics are Daisy, a Rambunctious Dog, Spirulina Products, Building a House, Hats and Bonnets, Horse and Buggy Days, Warehouse Information, Refrigeration Advantages, Kaleidoscopes, Video Selections, Composing Music, Bedspreads and Quilts, Fruits and Vegetables, Mysteries in Israel, T.V. Dinners and Frozen Foods, Attending Church, Diary Time, How to Use a Dictionary, The Pleiadians, Spiritual Predictions, Visual Apparitions, Soya Products, Living in a Rest Home and Vaudeville Entertainment.

ADVENTUROUS EXPERIENCES is a worthwhile book with many stimulating topics, stories and articles.

Cecelia Frances Page has published five, original screenplays and three, original, poetry books. The original screenplays are entitled <u>Walking in the Light</u>, <u>Flashbacks</u>, <u>Celestial Connections I and II</u> and <u>Adventures in Lemuria I and II</u>. The three, original, poetry books are entitled <u>Cosmic Dimensions</u>, <u>Vivid Impressions</u> and <u>Significant Introspections</u>. Cecelia Frances Page has written over five hundred, original poems. Several of her poems are published in <u>The World's Best Poems of 2004 and 2005</u>.

Cecelia has been writing since the age of 19. She has written 41 books. Some of her books published by iUniverse are entitled: <u>Westward Pursuit</u>, <u>Opportune Times</u>, <u>Imagine If…</u>, <u>Fortunately</u>, <u>Mystical Realities</u>, <u>Magnificent Celestial Journeys</u>, <u>Extraordinary Encounters</u>, <u>Brilliant Candor</u>, <u>Expand Your Awareness</u>, <u>Seek Enlightenment Within</u>, <u>Vivid Memories of Halcyon</u>, <u>Awaken to Spiritual Illumination</u>, <u>Adventures on Ancient Continents</u>, <u>Pathways to Spiritual Realization</u>, <u>Celestial Connections</u>, <u>Phenomenal Experiences</u>, <u>Celestial Beings from Outer Space</u>, <u>Awesome Episodes</u>, <u>Incredible Times,</u> <u>Interpretations of Life</u>, <u>New Perspectives</u>, <u>Tremendous Moments</u>, <u>Amazing Stories and Articles</u>, <u>Horizons Beyond</u>, <u>Fascinating Topics</u>, <u>Certain People Make A Difference,</u> <u>Amazing Stories and Articles</u>, <u>Power of Creative and Worthwhile Living</u>, <u>Tangible Realities,</u> <u>Extraterrestrial Civilizations on Earth</u>, <u>Adventurous Experiences,</u> <u>Relevant Interests</u> and more.

Cecelia Frances Page has a B.A. and M.A. in Education with a focus in English, Speech and Psychology. Cecelia is an excellent pianist. She is a piano and voice teacher, author, educator, philosopher, photographer and artist. Cecelia believes that creative abilities and talents can be achieved. Cecelia Frances Page continues to write more, worthwhile books to inspire her readers.

ONE

STEVE OMAR, A WORLD TRAVELER

Steve Omar, who grew up in San Clemente in Southern California, is a world traveler. He has traveled with very little money. Steve Omar has traveled into the Himalayan Mountains into Kashmir and India. He has traveled to Australia, New Zealand, Africa, Iceland, Fiji, Tahiti, Samoa, Morea, Bali, Hawaii, Java, the Bahamas, Puerto Rico, Japan, East and West Indies, 13 countries in Europe, the U.S.A., Mexico, South America and more.

Steven Omar traveled lightly. He lived in Maui in the Hawaiian Islands for nearly forty years. He encountered many dangers when he traveled to the Middle East. He dressed in clothing of each country so he wouldn't appear to be an American. He actually disguised himself in order not to be noticed by the people who lived in the Middle East.

Steve traveled on foot, by bus and he hitchhiked. He was able to communicate with different people while he was traveling. He learned foreign languages so he could speak to different people as he traveled. He tasted a variety of vegan foods which he selected from grocery stores, delicatessens and restaurants. He was invited to eat meals with people in their homes. He ate many authentic dishes of raw and steamed vegetables, rice, home cooked, wheat bread and raw fruit. He drank coffee when it was available and carried bottled water with him while he traveled. Tap water usually wasn't safe to drink.

Steve describes the Himalayan Mountains as a diverse setting of rocks, crevices, wild flowers, grasses, slopes and peaceful atmosphere. Steve said, "The Himalayan Mountains are a paradise where I experienced peace. The trails and roads were narrow and many walking areas were difficult to climb."

Small, Himalayan villages were unique. There was no running water or electricity in many villages. The village people in the Himalayan Mountains were usually friendly but also timid and shy.

Steve discovered ancient ruins in the Andes Mountains. He stopped at religious shrines and village temples. He was able to sit in a Buddha position to pray and meditate. He witnessed Andes people sitting near shrines and in temples praying quietly.

In the Middle East Steve Omar went to Egypt. He dressed as an Egyptian to fit in with the Egyptian people. He sat in mosques and Egyptian temples. He ate Egyptian eggplant dishes, vegan shish kebabs strung together. He ate mostly raw vegetables and fruits.

Hotels were expensive to stay in. Steve stayed in simple rooms with many other travelers in order to save money. He slept on buses. He went by foot frequently and walked long distances. The terrain in Egypt was changeable. Palm trees and other desert plants were spread out along dry landscapes in Egypt. The Nile River was picturesque. Steve walked near the Nile River embankments. The water is a vivid, deep blue color. The Nile River flows for hundreds of miles through Egypt. Tourists travel by boat on the Nile River to different villages and cities. Some people swim in the Nile River.

Steve Omar went to the famous Giza pyramid. This enormous pyramid was made of tons of stones which had to be built stone by stone by Egyptian workers thousands of years ago. The builders used a specific plan to build each pyramid. Steve walked into the Giza pyramid. It was very hot and it felt like a heated oven inside. The temperature was at least 150 degrees deep in the interior of the pyramid. Steve did not stay in the pyramid very long because of the extreme heat.

Steve rode a camel in the Sahara Desert to the Sphinx and Great Pyramid. Steve went to an ancient village made of sandstone. Villagers rode donkeys and camels. There were no motor vehicles. Everyone was dressed in turbans, robes and sandals. Women wore veils, long black dresses and burkas. He could only see their eyes. There was no technology in 2004.

Steve Omar went to Alexandria and the rebuilt library of Alexandria. Gourmet, Egyptian food was inexpensive. Steve stayed in an ocean view hotel for only $5.00 a night. There were no other Americans.

Steve Omar encountered dangers in Kashmir near the Pakistan border especially on public buses. There were five Western Caucasians on the public bus Omar traveled in. The Al Qaida made the five Western travelers, including Steve Omar, get off the bus. They were carefully inspected at the bus station.

A Kashmir inspector asked Steve Omar where he was from and why he came to Kashmir. Steve Omar said he was an American journalist. The inspector liked Steve's last name, Omar. He took Steve Omar's dark glasses and kept them. Steven Omar was allowed to enter Kashmir. The Al Qaida militia were invading Kashmir at the time. Steve had to be careful because it was dangerous in Kashmir.

The sacred ruins in Peru were fascinating to Steve Omar. He experienced a very high vibration in Machu Picchu. Inca priests prayed before the mountainsides for sunlight and rain. They prayed to the nature gods and deities regularly. They presented fruit and lit candles to the gods. They rang bells and chanted powerfully as they called to their gods and deities.

Steve Omar mingled among the Inca Indians in Machu Picchu. They dressed in colorful, llama woven blankets and hand sewn, colorful hats. They dressed very warmly because of the cold climate in the high mountains. The Inca Indians were short, light brown, skinned people. They spoke the Inca language and some Spanish.

Steve Omar was friendly to the Inca Indians. He learned about their ancient culture. Their customs were sacred. They believed in equality and in their nature gods and deities. Steve visited some thick, clay walled dwellings. The Incans built one square dwelling on another with no windows.

All inhabitants in Machu Picchu were women in ancient times. The women invited men into Machu Picchu once a year to mate with the women. Machu Picchu was a very peaceful place according to Steve Omar. Steve went to the sacred valley of the Incas. There were temples and other buildings that were giant size. Steve's Inca Indian guide said these temples and buildings were built by Atlanteans.

Steve Omar went to Lima, Peru, where Indians robbed tourists. He lived with local people. He saw Inca artifacts and beautiful jewelry. He went into a Spanish Cathedral where he saw ancient, oil paintings from the Conquistadores from the 1500s.

Steve Omar went up into the Andes over 14,000 feet where there was very little oxygen. Few people could survive there. Steve did yoga, breathing exercises and chewed cocoa leaves with the Indians. The cocoa leaves strengthened him.

Lake Titicaca is the sacred lake of Incas at the border of Peru and Bolivia. Steve went in a boat across the lake into Bolivia. The Indians live on floating, artificial islands woven by reeds. They float around on their floating islands.

Steve Omar went to the seaport of Copacabana, which is an exotic, Indian village on the Bolivian border near Lake Titicaca. Under lake water is a prehistoric, ruined city. Steve stayed in a primitive, Peruvian village called Puno.

A revolution broke out in Puno. Steve Omar escaped in time on the only highway back to Lima. He went to the most exciting, amazing city ever found in South America and the world called Tijuanaco. Tijuanaco is the oldest city in the world. Archaeologists believe Tijuanaco existed 26,000 years ago. Temples, pyramids, canals, wharves near a seaport existed. There are statues and carvings of all the races. It appears that space people had advanced spacesuits on. The buildings were made of very heavy stones which cannot be lifted by modern cranes. Steve was very impressed with the way the heavy stones were fitted together. The local Indians said the stones were flown in the air by some special energy from spaceships.

Tijuanaco experienced severe earthquakes and it was not destroyed. Only the Spanish Cathedrals and buildings were destroyed. The heavy stones were indestructible because they were pieced very tightly together.

Steve Omar saw elephants and monkeys on huge highways in India. He went into Buddhist and Hindu temples. He witnessed Brahma bulls and cows that slept on the highways. New Delhi, the capital city, was crowded. There were old buildings built by the British and Hindus.

Monkeys chased parliament politicians out of the buildings so they could not perform their parliament duties. Gangs of monkeys robbed grocery stores and robbed people in the streets. Monkeys are considered sacred in India.

Elephants robbed grocery stores and breweries. They became drunk. Holy men sit on the sidewalks. People give them food so they stayed alive. Jains carry brooms to sweep insects away. They do not believe in killing any insects.

When Steve Omar took Indian taxis to hotels he paid the taxi drivers in advance for a specific distance. In this way the taxi drivers could not charge too much. They accepted rupees for payment. Steve Omar stayed in a hotel that did not have air conditioning. The temperature was 120 degrees. He was very hot and dehydrated.

Steve Omar went into the Himalayan Mountains in India. He saw beautiful, pine tree forests. Steve came to the Valley of Vale in Kashmir. He saw floating and hanging gardens, mystical forests and snow capped mountain peaks. There were yellow poppies in meadows for miles. The fresh mountain air was so refreshing and uplifting. Steve swam across the Dal Lake which was sacred. Villagers on the mainland cheered Steve for swimming so far across the sacred lake. He came to Srinigar. In 2001 Srinigar was a very dangerous place. Steve dressed like an Arab. Friends rescued Steve and took him to the floating palace on a sacred island on the sacred lake in Kashmir. Steve Omar stayed in the palace for eight days. Kings, queens, princes, princesses and most world leaders have stayed in this palace. Steve traveled back to Maui in Hawaii by plane. He arrived in Maui with no money. He hitchhiked to his home in Lahaina.

Steve Omar traveled to approximately forty American states. He hitchhiked 6,000 miles from Florida to Maine. He also used a car to travel around the U.S.A. He traveled from California to Arizona through deserts with yucca trees and desert animals such as snakes, toads and jack rabbits. He continued through New Mexico through more dry lands and deserts. He went through woods, cattle land and clay built towns. He toured through Roswell known for extraterrestrial contacts in New Mexico.

Texas was enormous, yet dry with more cattle land, oil wells, small towns and large cities such as Dallas and Houston. Houston had a water canal with terraces on either side. Small outdoor cafes with tables were near the blue, water canal.

New Orleans in Louisiana was built with French buildings with green shutters and brick walls. There were many musical groups performing in bars, cafes and other places. The night life was very exciting. Jazz bands and singers performed all night every night of the week. Steve ate French food. There was dancing in the streets and parties going on.

In Florida Steve Omar went surfing during a hurricane. He survived enormous waves. He was brave to surf in dangerous weather. He worked at a ranch in the Everglades which was filled with alligators and poisonous snakes. Quicksand swallowed up cars. Even small houses sank in quicksand sinkholes. He survived in dangerous, lightning storms.

Steve Omar traveled by bus from San Diego, California to Costa Rica. He explored jungles in Costa Rica. There was a war going on in Guatemala in 1969 when he arrived there. He could not hitchhike because he would have been killed. He avoided going by train. He went in a bus filled with Guatemalan soldiers. He sat in the back of the bus. Another man volunteered to become Steve Omar's bodyguard to protect him. He survived by hiding out in a hotel. He remained calm during a street fight.

Steve Omar managed to keep traveling through Central America during a war going on. He eventually went back to California. He spoke Spanish when he encountered people in Mexico and Central America so he could communicate with them. He continued to travel around the world to fascinating places.

An isolated beach in Panama was quite long. Steve Omar slept on this isolated beach for a week. No one else came to this beach. Steve was by himself the whole week. It rained every afternoon and the evening air was warm all night.

Steve Omar continued to travel to more interesting destinations in the world. He went to Canada, South America and Mexico. Then he went back to Maui in the Hawaiian Islands.

TWO

ADVENTURES AT THE GREAT LAKES

Stewart and Marla Thompson were newlyweds. They decided to explore the Great Lakes in the Northeast of America, which are lakes Ontario, Erie, Huron, Michigan and Superior. They prepared for their adventure by renting a cruising boat which had one cabin with a kitchenette. They packed the boat with food and camping equipment.

Stewart and Marla lived in Rochester in New York State. They were used to many conveniences and household items. They would have to adjust to life on a boat while they sailed from one great lake to another. The sails had to be checked for rips before the journey. Fruit and vegetables were stored in shelves in the kitchenette. Milk, butter, cheese, sliced lunch meat, eggs and juice were stored in a refrigerator.

Shortly after their wedding day the Thompsons set sail on Lake Ontario. This lake was close to Rochester, New York. The lake was very deep and swift. The Thompsons put up the sails in their boat. The wind blew through the sails causing the boat to move across the lake.

Stewart and Marla enjoyed the rippling blue water on Lake Ontario, which is farther northeast in America. This lake has a lot of fresh water.

They witnessed Canadian ducks in the lake water. Ducks bobbed up and down in the rippling water.

Stewart and Marla decided to fish for trout and perch in Lake Ontario. Stewart caught three trout and several perch. Marla cleaned each fish. She put three of the five fish in the refrigerator to keep them cool. She cut and cleaned two trout to cook for dinner. She cooked the sliced trout over open flames until they were ready to eat.

Marla prepared steamed potatoes and a green salad with dark green lettuce, sliced tomatoes and carrots. She added sliced, green peppers and parsley. A vinaigrette dressing was added to spice up the salad. Marla put homemade, rye bread on the small, dining room table. She put salad in salad dishes and placed the two salads on the table. The fish was put on two, larger plates. Steamed potatoes with basil were added to each plate.

It was time to eat before the fish and potatoes got cold. The savory fish, potatoes and salad were delicious and nutritious. For dessert Marla and Stewart ate fresh, sliced pears. They drank hot, herb tea during their meal. They cleaned up after eating.

It began to become dark. The moon came out over Lake Ontario. The light of the Moon shone across the lake. Beams of light reflected in the lake. Marla and Stewart sat on deck and watched the moonlight as Stewart played his guitar. This setting was very romantic and beautiful.

Marla and Stewart slept in a double bed on the boat in their cabin that night. They exchanged passionate embraces and consummated their marriage. Both of them experienced blissful feelings. They listened to the wind howling near the lake. They slept warm under the blankets.

The next morning Stewart got up first. He saw seagulls flying overhead near the boat. Some of the seagulls landed on the deck and sail rims. Some seagulls made bird sounds. Marla woke up when she heard seagulls making loud, sharp, shrill sounds. After breakfast Stewart directed the boat to the Niagara Falls which was West.

Once the boat approached Niagara Falls Stewart and Marla witnessed many rivers coming together to form waterfalls. The waterfalls were very high, swift and they produced a lot of mist. Stewart and Marla put on raincoats and rain hats to keep mist off their clothes and bodies.

Stewart and Marla sailed into the river at Niagara Falls. They saw rainbows gleaming from the mist. Tons of water was flowing from the many waterfalls. Rainbow colors were reflected in each waterfall. These waterfalls were the most beautiful waterfalls on Earth. Marla and Stewart were amazed and quite impressed when they saw multiple, reflecting rainbows. Later they watched a crimson-purple sunset near dusk.

The Thompsons went to Lake Erie next. Lake Erie was close to Ohio. Lake Erie was larger than Lake Ontario. They sailed across this lake through swift currents and gales. They encountered flocks of different birds flying across the lake. Some were ducks and geese fluttering around and dipping in the lake water.

Marla and Stewart enjoyed the cool breezes while they sailed in their rented boat. They pulled the sails down at night so the boat would slow down at night while they were sleeping.

It began to rain heavily the second night Stewart and Marla were on Lake Erie. They stayed in their boat cabin. The boat began to rock a lot because of wind and rippling water. Rain splashed on deck and caused puddles of rain to drip everywhere. Marla and Stewart became worried. They dressed in their raincoats, hats and boots.

The Thompsons took buckets out on deck and scooped up puddles of rain water to throw overboard. They continued to remove more rain water from the boat. They continued scooping up rain water for hours until they became quite exhausted. It kept raining for some time.

Finally the rain subsided by early morning. Marla and Stewart went back into their cabin. They removed their raincoats, hats and boots. They went back to bed to rest and recuperate from the arduous effort to keep excess rain water off the boat. They slept for hours.

By midday Marla and Stewart got up and dressed warmly before going out on deck. The sun had finally appeared in the sky once the rain stopped. The Thompsons continued to sail across Lake Erie. They were relieved that the boat had not capsized.

Marla prepared more fish that she took out of the refrigerator. She baked perch and made rice pilaf and steamed, green beans. She buttered homemade bread. Hot coffee was prepared as well. Marla and Stewart enjoyed baked perch, rice pilaf and green beans with buttered bread for the midday meal. They were very hungry because they had exerted themselves during the night removing rain water from the boat.

The Thompsons continued to sail on Lake Huron and then Lake Michigan. These fresh water lakes were quite deep and large. Many memorable experiences occurred when the Thompsons sailed across five, great lakes in America on their honeymoon.

Three

Roving Around

Harry Putnam was a curious, adventurous person. While he was growing up he went hiking, mountain climbing, camping, swimming and bicycle riding. Harry was an outdoor person. He lived with his parents in Los Gatos, California.

Mountain climbing especially interested Harry. He went mountain climbing at Mount Whitney in Eastern California. Mount Whitney is 14,000 feet high. Harry dressed in mountain clothes and mountain boots. He went mountain climbing with his older brother, Joshua, who was eighteen. Harry was sixteen years old. They climbed to the top of Mount Whitney in two days and one night.

Harry observed plants and animals when he went exploring in forests and woods. Sword ferns, lichens on trunks and branches, grasses and four leaf clovers were interesting to notice. Harry watched brown squirrels, wild hares and raccoons scurry around in forest lands. He sat on a large log to observe the wild life in his visual surroundings. He spotted several deer grazing under silver spruce and pine trees. They chewed grass, lichens and tree leaves. The deer noticed Harry sitting on a log watching them. They continued to munch on grass, lichens and tree leaves. Harry continued to observe the forest life quietly for a period of time.

Harry went down to the beach to walk on the warm sand. He collected sand dollars, clam shells, scallop shells and nautilus shells. He listened to the sound of the ocean waves when he put his ear close to a nautilus shell. Harry watched seagulls, pelicans, sandpipers and small, brown birds walking in groups on wet sand near the ocean. Many seabirds left bird feet designs on the sand.

Turtles were intriguing to observe. Harry watched giant and regular size green and gray-brown turtles walking on beach sand to lay their turtle eggs. Mother turtles dug big holes to bury hundreds of eggs. The sand keeps the turtle eggs warm. Turtles break out of their shells within days. Baby turtles try to find the ocean. Turtles find food in the ocean.

Harry sat on the warm sand on the beach and watched baby turtles racing to the ocean. Seagulls swooped down and grabbed baby turtles. They flew away with the turtles. Baby turtles who survived swam deep into the ocean. Some of these turtles were eaten by sharks and other, larger fish.

Harry liked to explore in remote places. He went with his older brother, Joshua to the Mojave Desert. They decided to camp in the desert near some yucca trees. White yucca flowers were blooming in these desert trees. The yucca trees silhouetted against the desert sky. The flowers on the yucca trees sent out an unusual fragrance.

Joshua and Harry set up two tents. They placed tent, wood stakes in the desert sand. Canvas was pulled up with ropes which Joshua and Harry tied to the wood stakes in the ground. Once the tents were put up Joshua and Harry put their bedrolls in their tents. Camping equipment was stored in the tents.

Harry and Joshua began walking into the desert to look around. It was springtime. So the weather was not as hot as in the summertime. They strolled past more yucca trees, desert shrubs and small, desert plants. They saw desert snakes slithering on desert sand. Small desert toads crawled on rocks. Desert spiders hid in the shade of desert rocks. Spiders crawled into the open to catch smaller insects.

Some desert animals lurked behind desert shrubs. Some coyotes were in the distance looking for food in the desert. Coyotes eat small rodents and desert birds, birds' eggs and desert berries from desert bushes. Coyotes roam about in small groups. Harry and Joshua saw six coyotes. Two coyotes were babies who followed their mothers.

Harry and Joshua observed the coyotes to study their behavior. They noticed the mother coyotes lie down so the baby coyotes could nurse. Two, male coyotes kept searching for berries, eggs and rodents. They dug into the sand to search for rodents that dwelled in underground tunnels.

Harry and Joshua observed one of the male coyotes chase off after a small rodent. It finally captured the rodent. The coyote killed the rodent. It began eating it. The other, male coyote ran over to the coyote that had captured the rodent. This coyote tried to eat part of the rodent. The first coyote grit its teeth and glared at the second coyote. It made a fierce, growling sound. It scared the second coyote away. This coyote went on eating the rodent.

It was beginning to get dark because the sun was going down. Harry and Joshua walked back to their camp. Joshua collected dry, desert sticks. Harry dug a campfire. They placed sticks in to the campfire area. Joshua lit the dry, desert branchlets. A burning campfire was established. The teenagers cooked hamburger in a skillet with cut onions and sliced potatoes. Harry added some tomato ketchup into the hamburger to create a better flavor in the meat.

When the hamburger was cooked and the onions and potatoes were properly cooked, Harry put cooked hamburger patties on hamburger buns. He added mustard and pickles on each bun. The sautéed onions and potatoes were added on two plates with each hamburger.

Harry and Joshua were hungry. The food was ready to eat. They sat on the sandy ground near the campfire to eat their prepared food. Harry thought the hamburger was very tasty. He put more tomato ketchup on his hamburger. The pickles and ketchup brought out the juicy flavor in the meat.

After Joshua and Harry were finished eating their hamburgers, onions and potatoes, they sat by the blazing fireplace to keep warm. The blazing fire kept it lighter near them. The sun was setting in the West. Magnificent colors were emerging in the Western sky near the horizon. Harry and Joshua notice the hues of crimson, orange-red and yellow colors "painted" in the sky.

Harry and Joshua observed the magnificent sunset until it got quite dark. The fire embers sparkled in the dark. It was time to clean up and they put the rest of the food away in containers. The containers were kept in a larger, storage container. They were sealed shut so wild animals couldn't get in. The larger container was locked in the trunk of their car.

Harry and Joshua looked at the stars and moon in the sky for a few minutes. Then they said goodnight. They got into their tents and zipped them up. They got into their bedrolls in order to go to sleep. During the night Harry and Joshua heard coyotes howling in the distance. They finally fell asleep.

During the night mountain cats and coyotes wandered near their campsite. The campfire was nearly out. The mountain cats sniffed around the two tents. Several of the mountain cats came over to the car and scratched their claws on the trunk lid. They could smell the food inside the trunk.

Harry woke up when he heard the mountain cats scratching on the car. He took his flashlight and opened his tent. He pointed his flashlight towards the mountain cats. He flashed the bright flashlight into the eyes of several mountain cats known as cougars. He yelled, "Shoo! Shoo! Shoo!" The cougars finally ran away.

Joshua woke up and came out of his tent with his flashlight. He spoke to Harry. He asked, "What is going on?" Harry replied, "Some cougars came into our campsite! I guess they were looking for food. They are gone now." Joshua said, "Let's go back in our tents to sleep. I hope we don't encounter any more disturbances!"

Harry and Joshua went back into their tents. They finally went back to sleep. The next day they prepared some breakfast. They fried eggs, bacon, hash browns and made pancakes. There was orange juice in the storage chest. After breakfast they cleaned up the campsite and made sure the fire was out.

While packing the car Joshua and Harry noticed scratches on the back of the car. Joshua said, "The cougars sure left their marks on our car!" Harry answered, "We can paint the car over when we get home."

Joshua and Harry headed back through the Mojave Desert past the yucca trees, shrubs and dry, desert land. Joshua drove the four door sedan for many miles. He came to a crossroad. The sign said, "Los Gatos." He turned right at the sign. He drove towards Los Gatos to go home to their parents' home.

Once Joshua and Harry were home they unpacked the car. They told their parents about their experiences in the Mojave Desert. Mr. Putnam noticed the scratches on his car. He frowned and said, "Who did this?!" Harry smiled and replied, "Would you believe it if I told you cougars scratched the car!" Mr. Putnam responded, "Please paint over these scratches." Harry replied, "We intend to repaint the car." Nothing more was said about the car.

Harry and Joshua purchased some car paint. They smoothed down the scratches on the car. They repainted the family car. It looked much better. There were no signs of scratches on the car once the car was repainted. Harry and Joshua decided not to camp in the Mojave Desert again. They continued to rove around to other remote places when they had the opportunity.

Four

ANTIA, AN UNDERWATER CITY

Underwater cities exist around the world in the ocean. Underwater cities were built by extraterrestrial beings from outer space. These space beings were capable of creating advanced looking cities with transparent substance.

A very modern, looking, underwater city existed near Puerto Rico deep in the ocean called Antia. Transparent domes were spread around with water streets between domes in Antia. Some buildings were towers. Some buildings looked like cathedrals with spiral designs and geometric patterns.

Fish and sharks were moving around near the domes, towers and cathedrals under the ocean. Human-like people lived in the underwater city in the domes and towers. Large windows existed in the domes.

Extraterrestrial human-like people were 4 feet, 5 feet and 6 feet tall. They were wearing silk, tight gowns and beautiful outfits which were purple, gold, white and turquoise. The space men and women mingled together. They were happy in this underwater city under the ocean.

There were no guns and nuclear weapons. These people lived in peace and harmony.

Translucent tunnels were connected to the domes, towers and cathedrals. The people walked through the tunnels from one dome to another dome. They could see the ocean surrounding the tunnels. They could observe the deep, ocean floor in the tunnels. Many ocean algae and plankton plus colorful corals were on the ocean floor. The deep ocean was beautiful and filled with sea life.

Many activities were taking place in the domes. People were playing games, singing, swimming in indoor pools and making arts and crafts. Some people were sitting in chairs at geometric tables. They were drinking fruit drinks and some were eating raw fruit. They socialized while they ate.

The extraterrestrial beings came to Earth from Astara in the Pleiades. They built their underwater city in the deep ocean where it was safe. Earth people went unaware that this underwater city was located near Puerto Rico deep in the ocean.

Life in the underwater city of Antia was blissful and peaceful. Then, one day a Navy submarine was navigating in the deep ocean near Puerto Rico. This Navy submarine came near the underwater city. Navy men looked out portholes and certain windows. They were surprised and shocked to witness this underwater city in the ocean.

The Navy Captain of the Navy submarine was informed about this underwater city. The Navy Captain looked through windows at the underwater city. He was amazed at the many, advanced, looking structures. He noticed human-like people walking in tunnels. There was a central plaza with gold statues of gods in the center of the underwater city.

The Navy Captain felt it was his duty to report what he witnessed. He decided to call the President of the United States to inform him about the underwater city. The President's secretary answered the phone. The Navy Captain said, "Hello. I would like to speak to the President please." The secretary replied, "The President is very busy right now. Can I take a message?" The Navy Captain said, "This is an emergency! I need to report an urgent matter!" The secretary replied, "Please state your message. I will give it to the President."

The Navy Captain said, "I am reporting an underwater city near Puerto Rico. The President needs to know about this amazing, underwater city. Please tell him what I witnessed. This underwater city has many, advanced, looking structures and tunnels!" The secretary said, "I'll have the President call you. What is your name and phone number?" The Navy Captain replied, "My name is Captain Shelby. My phone number is 1-555-527-0001. Be sure the President calls me. My submarine is near this underwater city right now." The secretary said, "I will notify the President right away. Goodbye." Captain Shelby said, "Goodbye."

Captain Shelby waited for the President to call back. He continued to observe the underwater city through the windows in the submarine. He saw lights on through the dome and tower windows. The lights were bright in the underwater city. The Navy crew observed the underwater city.

The extraterrestrial people in Antia, the underwater city, were able to see the navy submarine. A leader in Antia was concerned about the submarine near the underwater city. He decided to turn on an electrical device to seal the city from harm. The extraterrestrial beings were alerted about the submarine. They went about with their activities once the electric shield was on.

The President of the U.S.A. finally called Captain Shelby back. He said, "Hello. This is President Furman. Is this Captain Shelby?" Captain Shelby replied, "Yes. I want to report an underwater city near Puerto Rico on the ocean floor. It is made up of domes, towers and other structures."

President Furman said, "Have you seen extraterrestrials at this underwater city?" Captain Shelby replied, "Yes. They walk through tunnels from one dome to another dome and to the towers." President Furman asked, "Have they attacked your submarine yet?" Captain Shelby replied, "No. I think these extraterrestrials know we are observing them." President Furman spoke. "Stay where you are. If you notice any signs of danger withdraw quickly from the area. I will send more submarines to Puerto Rico. They will alert you when they have arrived."

Captain Shelby said, "Alright. I will wait for more submarines to arrive." The President said, "Be careful. Don't use any nuclear weapons at this time. You will be instructed what to do. Keep me informed if changes take place regarding your safety in your submarine." Captain Shelby replied, "Yes, I will contact you immediately." The President and submarine captain hung up their phones.

Captain Shelby and his Navy crew continued to observe the underwater city. If anything changed they would take action. Meanwhile, the Antians in the underwater city remained invisibly sealed off from any physical attacks from the American submarine.

The American submarine remained in the same location for several days and nights. The submarine was sent up to the surface for air whenever necessary. Within two days at least nine more submarines traveled to Puerto Rico in the Southern Hemisphere in the ocean.

Once there were ten submarines near Puerto Rico the President of the U.S.A. was notified. He instructed the captains to have the Navy crew send nuclear bombs and torpedoes to the underwater city to blow up this underwater domain.

The captains gave their commands. The torpedoes were sent swiftly to the underwater city of Antia. The torpedoes were unable to penetrate the electric shield around every section of the city. The captains and crew became aware that their weapons were useless. The city of Antia was protected by a magnetic shield.

Captain Shelby contacted President Furman by phone. He told the President that weapons could not penetrate the underwater city. The President, captains and crewmen realized that they could not destroy Antia deep under the ocean.

The Antians from Astara, in the Pleiades, continued to live under the ocean in their magnificent city.

FIVE

DAISY, A RAMBUNCTIOUS DOG

Daisy was a Scotch terrier. She had brownish-beige hair. Some bristly hair hung over her eyes. She was an energetic, high-strung dog. Daisy liked to bark and jump up on anyone who entered the house where Daisy lived.

Daisy was the only dog in the household. She was pampered and given a lot of attention. Daisy liked to stand on her hind legs to show off. She liked all the attention she could receive day by day. At night she fell asleep in her dog bed in a big basket near the living room couch.

Mary Frasher was Daisy's owner. Mary bought Daisy in a pet store downtown. Daisy cost $250.00. Mary paid the $250.00 and took Daisy home. Mary had purchased Daisy six months ago. Daisy was adjusted to her new home. She knew where her food was stored in the house. She was used to her bed.

Daisy had to be trained to go outdoors to go potty. She was also trained indoors to go potty in a specific place in a potty tray. Daisy finally learned to go potty properly in the house.

One day when Mary Frasher was away from the house Daisy had to wait alone. Daisy felt lonely and frustrated being alone. She barked and barked. This barking annoyed the nearby neighbors. Daisy continued to bark. She missed her owner, Mary Frasher.

Mary came home at 5:30 p.m. that day. When she opened the front door Daisy was there waiting for Mary. Daisy jumped up and touched Mary with her front paws. She whimpered while she touched Mary with her claws. Mary knew Daisy was glad to see her.

Daisy managed to jump up into Mary's arms. She licked Mary on the face affectionately. Her eyes sparkled with light. She was feeling much better now that Mary was home. Daisy depended on Mary to be her companion. Mary had cared for Daisy from the day they met.

Mary Frasher worked from Monday to Friday from 8:00 a.m. until 5:00 p.m. It took thirty minutes to get home after work. She had no one who could stay with her dog, Daisy while she was gone. Daisy found it difficult to be by herself. She had no one to play with when she was alone. She expected to receive attention.

Mary decided to have Daisy bred with a male, Scottish terrier. Daisy became pregnant. Within six months Daisy gave birth to four, baby puppies. This kept Daisy occupied because she looked after her four puppies.

While Mary was away from the house Daisy allowed her puppies to nurse for food. Daisy licked her puppies to keep them clean. The puppies continued to grow. They played with each other while they grew stronger and stronger. Daisy watched them play. She was no longer lonely because she was surrounded by her puppies. She stopped barking incessantly. She had settled down now that she was a mother.

Six

SCAMMER TRAGEDIES

Many scammers advertise on the Internet. They use well known names of wealthy people to fool their vulnerable victims. Generally, elderly people believe they can receive millions of dollars from scammers.

Tim Winston was eighty years old. He was a retired college professor. Tim read about sweepstakes on his Internet. He thought he could receive $5 million. He was asked to fill out a sweepstakes form. He was required to mention his full name, social security number, residential and mailing addresses, phone numbers, his occupation and all bank accounts, etc.

Tim answered all required questions. He e-mailed all the information to the sweepstakes scammers. He was told to pay $750.00. So, Tim sent $750.00 by Western Union. Once the scammers received $750.00 Tim waited to receive the $5 million dollars. He was told the money would arrive by check within ten days.

Tim waited for the check to be sent by a courier to Tim's residence. Ten days went by. The courier didn't arrive with the check. Tim contacted the sweepstakes representative. The representative told Tim that the courier had an accident during delivery. He was killed. So the check was lost.

The scammer representative said he would wire the $5 million dollars to Tim's bank account. He said the money would be sent within five days. Tim waited to receive the wired check. Five days went by and the wired check arrived at Tim's bank. Tim went to the bank to get some money out from the wired check. He was told that the $5 million dollar check was not accepted by the bank. The check was not worth anything.

Tim wrote the sweepstakes representative on his computer. He complained that the wired check was not valid. He told the scammer that he wanted his $750.00 back. The representative wrote back and said the check should have been accepted by the bank. Tim was not refunded his $750.00.

Tim decided to try another sweepstakes contest. He picked another well known name. He was told to pay $550.00 first. Tim paid $550.00 at Western Union. The money was sent immediately by Western Union. Tim was promised $2.5 million dollars. He was supposed to receive the money within seven days. This time Tim hoped he would receive $2.5 million dollars. Seven days passed. The $2.5 million dollars came in a check at Tim's front door. A courier presented the check. Tim signed a paper to receive the check.

Tim opened the sweepstakes check. It looked authentic. It was written out to Tim Winston for $2.5 million dollars. Tim was excited when he read this check. The next day he took the $2.5 million dollar check to his bank. He planned to deposit the money in his bank account. The bank teller looked at the check carefully. She took the check to the bank manager.

The bank manager examined the sweepstakes check very carefully. She detected that certain numbers were wrong. She called someone who was an expert about fraudulent checks. The bank manager said the sweepstakes check was fraudulent. The bank manager brought the worthless check back to Tim. She told Tim that the check was fraudulent. It could not be deposited in the bank.

Tim was angry and extremely disappointed. He kept on entering more sweepstakes contests. He sent his savings to risk winning. He kept losing money. He never received any money from the Internet sweepstakes.

Tim was living on a Social Security payment sent once a month. He had very little savings in case of emergencies. He experienced one scam after another scam which caused him to become broke. Tim refused to listen to advice from friends and relatives. He gambled his money away by risking his money when he paid fees to receive sweepstakes funds.

---------- SEVEN ----------

AFRICAN ADVENTURES

Africa is a country with many contrasts and weather changes. Africa has savannahs, dense jungles, deserts and coastal resorts. Many Africans still live in small villages created by the village people.

Adventures are evident in jungles, savannahs and even in remote locations of Africa. Tourists go to Africa to observe jungle animals and tropical birds. They are able to witness the behavior of lions, tigers, elephants, monkeys, apes, tropical birds, crocodiles, alligators, hyenas, gazelles and baboons, etc.

Jim and Anita Thornburg arranged a trip to Africa to The Congo. They planned to photograph and produce videos of wildlife they encountered on their adventures in the jungles and savannahs of South Africa.

The Thornburgs camped out as they journeyed to wild and remote areas in The Congo. They had a jeep to travel in. They packed the jeep with tents, boxes of camping equipment and some food such as raw vegetables, fruit, bread and some canned goods. They brought cooking tools and matches. The Thornburgs were prepared to cook during their journey in The Congo and other places.

Once Jim and Anita Thornburg came to Leopoldville on southwest of The Congo they stayed in a hotel overnight in order to relax and to enjoy modern conveniences before they went into jungles to camp outdoors. There was television and restaurant food at the hotel, which was air-conditioned.

The next day Jim and Anita repacked their jeep. They drove northeast into a large, jungle area. They were in a dense section of the jungle. They heard the sounds of jungle animals. There were black panthers, tigers, spider monkeys, baboons, jungle snakes and a variety of insects.

While Jim and Anita were walking through the dense jungle they encountered a large, cobra snake moving in a tree above them. The cobra saw them. It darted its head towards them. The tongue of the cobra stuck out and dangled back and forth towards Jim and Anita as they walked by. The Thornburgs were glad to move away from the long, thick snake without being harmed.

When Jim and Anita continued their stroll into the dense jungle they heard growling sounds from a black panther. The black panther appeared in a tree branch near them. It continued to growl fiercely at them. Jim and Anita became frightened. They began running as fast as they could to get away from the panther.

The panther remained in the tree where it had been staying. Evidently it was not hungry enough to chase after Jim and Anita. They kept running through jungle foliage and swampy areas. They had to be careful to avoid water snakes and crocodiles in the swampy areas.

Jim and Anita came to a waterfall near a jungle grotto. The waterfall was beautiful, fresh water. Jim and Anita needed to rest and cool off. The pool of water below the waterfall looked clean and safe. They decided to go in the pool to swim and to cool off. They took off most of their clothing and went into the pool of water. The water was cool and refreshing. They were able to relax and recuperate.

After swimming for a period of time Jim and Anita were rested and they put their clothes back on. It was time to leave the jungle before it got too dark at sundown. Jim and Anita walked back in the direction they had come from. It took more time to go back through the jungle.

Rain began to fall heavily in the jungle. Jim and Anita kept walking in the jungle. They became sopping wet from the dripping rain. Then the sun went down. Jim and Anita had to walk in the dark. They passed wet spider webs with big spiders crawling in their webs. The Thornburgs were lost. They couldn't find their jeep.

A tiger was hiding in the jungle. It saw Jim and Anita walking in the dark. The tiger growled loudly and gritted its teeth and glared with its piercing eyes at Jim and Anita. They stood still for a minute or two. They were very frightened when they saw the tiger, which was bright orange-brown with spots.

The tiger walked towards Jim and Anita. The Thornburgs decided to climb up a tall, jungle tree to escape from the tiger. They kept climbing higher and higher hoping to be safe in the sturdy tree.

The tiger came up to the jungle tree and growled again as it stared up at Jim and Anita. Jim located some solid cones in the tree. He grabbed some cones and threw one cone after another at the tiger to scare it away.

Jim and Anita stayed in the jungle tree and rested on sturdy branches for the rest of the night. The tiger finally left and went back into the jungle. The rain finally subsided before morning.

The next morning Jim and Anita woke up. They noticed that the tiger had disappeared. Jim and Anita decided to come out of the sturdy tree. Jim checked where the sun was in the sky. He knew their jeep was headed west. So, Jim and Anita walked west and after an hour they found their jeep at the edge of the jungle.

The Thornburgs drove to Uganda which was east of The Congo. It took all day to drive on a narrow, dirt road to the border of Uganda. They came to Lake Victoria, which was deep blue. Lake Victoria was named after Queen Victoria in England. The English people owned different provinces in Africa.

Jim and Anita rented a motorboat and went boating on Lake Victoria. The lake water was beautiful and enjoyable to move across. There were other boats on the lake. After boating at Lake Victoria Jim and Anita drove their rented jeep to Kenya which was east of Uganda.

The Thornburgs stopped in Nairobi to relax. They stayed overnight in an air-conditioned hotel. They ate exotic, African dishes of food at a restaurant at the hotel. They had steamed sweet potatoes, eggplant and gazelle meat which were spicy because the food was cooked in spicy herbs. They were served African coffee. A mixed, fruit dessert with tropical, jungle, fresh fruit was served. The Thornburgs drank bottled water imported from Europe.

After taking in cultural experiences in Nairobi such as African museums, art galleries and different, African restaurants the Thornburgs continued their journey to Mt. Kilimanjaro which was south of Nairobi. They planned to observe the gorillas that lived at this well known mountain.

Once Jim and Anita reached the foot of Mt. Kilimanjaro they parked their jeep near a dense jungle. They brought their camera and video, camera equipment with them as they walked into the dense jungle. They walked deep into the jungle.

Tropical birds were nesting in jungle trees. Some tropical birds were making their unusual, bird sounds. Then, suddenly they heard very strange, loud, haunting sounds in the distance. These strange sounds were made by gorillas.

Jim and Anita walked cautiously in the direction of the gorillas. Suddenly a large, male gorilla appeared out of the dense brush. It glared at Jim and Anita. It made fierce sounds and it pounded its chest. It was trying to establish its dominance and the gorilla was trying to scare Jim and Anita away.

The gorilla moved closer and closer to the Thornburgs. They stood very still. They knew that Jane Goodall, the famous anthropologist, had observed gorillas at Mt. Kilimanjaro. They waited for the male gorilla to calm down. They knew he was bluffing to scare them away.

Once the male gorilla calmed down other gorillas were visible. Mother gorillas with their babies were crawling on the ground. Mother gorillas were grooming their babies. Some baby gorillas were nursing. Other gorillas were gathering tree fruit to eat. Some gorillas were playing with other gorillas.

Jim and Anita sat quietly and observed the gorillas for hours. They noticed that dominant males guarded female gorillas. Baby gorillas were protected by male and female gorillas. The gorillas were living in a gorilla community. They knew how to stay clean. They knew how to gather food. They climbed in the jungle trees and slept in the trees.

Jim and Anita photographed the behavioral habits of the gorillas for a week. They camped out at night at the edge of the jungle. They prepared campfires and cooked meat, potatoes, vegetables and prepared coffee. They ate fresh, jungle fruit for breakfast and dessert.

The Thornburgs drove back to Nairobi. They took an air flight back to America to San Diego, California where they lived. They recalled their memories about their African adventures with a sense of worthwhile pursuit.

EIGHT

AWARENESS GROUP

A group entitled Awareness Group has been established 20 years ago. The Awareness Group meets at Round Table Pizza in Arroyo Grande, California. Homer Hoyt has been the leader of this stimulating group which meets from 7:00 p.m. to 9:00 p.m. on the second and fourth Tuesday of each month.

This Awareness Group is very worthwhile because many unusual topics are presented. There is a discussion before the presentation. Each person who presents a topic brings books and an outline to follow. Some presenters show videos on the fourth Tuesday.

Many topics have been presented at the Awareness Group through the years. Usually 12 to 15 people come to the Tuesday meetings. The following topics have been presented. UFO Sightings, Extraterrestrials from Outer Space, Indigo People, Underground Cities, Lemuria and Atlantis, The Red Sea, Conspiracies about U.S. Presidents, Inflation and Money, Ancient Races, Extraterrestrial Evidence in the Bible, Poetry to Listen To, Mysteries of the Bible and many more topics have been presented at the Awareness Group.

Participants in the Awareness Group ask questions and express their viewpoints about many issues and topics. People come from far away. They come from Atascadero, Morro Bay, Santa Maria, Cayucos, Lompoc, Arroyo Grande, Nipomo, etc. They are able to expand their awareness about many, unusual topics.

Nine

Horrendous Hurricanes

Hurricanes occur suddenly in different locations such as in Hawaii, Florida, South Carolina and in the Pacific Ocean. Hurricanes occur on the East Coast of America, Northeastern part of South America, Guam and Japan, etc.

Hurricanes are caused when very strong gusts of wind blow. It rains heavily. Wind swirls severely and destroys buildings and floods many acres of land.

New Orleans in Louisiana was severely hit by a massive hurricane approximately two years ago in 2006. The whole city was flooded. Many homes and public buildings were under rain water. Thousands of people were forced to leave their homes.

When the hurricane was over many restaurants, business establishments, churches, schools and other buildings were badly damaged. Hurricane winds are from 100 to 200 miles in their swiftness. Buildings fall down and blow apart.

New Orleans is still in a damaged condition. Many homes are being rebuilt or abandoned. The cost of rebuilding homes and public buildings is very expensive. Galveston in Texas was flooded in 2008. Again, many homes and public buildings were under rain water. Many people had to leave Galveston because their homes were destroyed by a fierce hurricane.

In 1982 an unexpected hurricane took place in the Hawaiian Islands. The weatherman said it was going to be a sunny, pleasant day. Many people went to the beach that day. Once they got to the beach they sat in the sand and went swimming.

A hurricane made a u-turn and headed back to Hawaii. Suddenly the hurricane blew into the Hawaiian Islands unexpectedly. Many people on the islands rushed away from the beach into the hotels. All the electricity went out.

People on the Hawaiian Islands were trapped in their hotels. All restaurants and shops were closed. Hotel rooms were dark. There was no food available. They weren't able to watch television or read books. People had to stay on their beds to keep away from the rain and fierce hurricane. Kauai was devastated by the hurricane.

Coconuts were flying everywhere and people had to avoid the danger of coconuts hitting them. Hard coconuts can cause serious accidents.

Ocean waves were at least 30 feet high. The waves crashed to shore. Beach dwellers had to rush to a safer place. Hotel rooms remained dark for three days. Tourists were uncomfortable and restless because they were unable to enjoy vacation activities such as restaurant food, swimming, surfing, sailing, snorkeling and sunbathing on the beach. They spent a lot of money to go to Hawaii just to stay indoors with nothing to do.

A hurricane called Iniki took place in 1991 in Lahaina on Maui in the Hawaiian Islands. Waves were 30 feet high. The ocean waves crashed to shore and rushed into beachfront restaurants and business establishments. Surfboards, snorkels, kayaks, sailboards and swim fins were totally destroyed by the hurricane.

Large, expensive yachts were capsized because of crashing waves. A pier near the Lahaina shore was blown in the turbulent, ocean waves. Several people were badly injured and several people were killed.

It took quite a while to restore Lahaina after the severe hurricane. Hurricanes are forecast today by weather detectors. At least people can prepare for hurricanes. Hurricanes usually cause a lot of damage. People need to save emergency money to use to repair their homes and businesses after a hurricane.

TEN

FLORIDA VACATIONLAND

Dan and Alisha Stromberg decided to go on a vacation in Florida in America. They lived in Minneapolis, Minnesota. They took an airflight to Tallahassee, the capital city of Florida. From the airport they took a taxi to a well known hotel to stay for several days and nights. Tallahassee means "old town" where Spaniards settled. Dan and Alisha attended the Museum of Florida History in Tallahassee. Mastodon bones and treasures from a sunken ship are among its highlights.

Dan and Alisha went to Florida in early Spring. They decided to take a motorboat into the swamps. They witnessed alligators swimming in the swamps. Trees were in the swamp with hanging lichen. Alligators swam near their boat. They were not used to these alligators. So, they were careful while navigating in the swamps.

Spanish, clay dwellings with reddish-brown tile roofs exist in Tallahassee. The capital building is a cathedral shaped, unique looking building. There were museums with historical artifacts, Indian jewelry and clothes to look at. Dan and Alisha gazed at many Indian collections worth observing.

Dan and Alisha went to Wakulla Springs outside Tallahassee which is 185 feet deep. It is one of America's deepest springs. Dan and Alisha rented a car in Tallahassee. They drove southwest in the northern section of Florida to Pensacola. Pensacola is a college town with beautiful beaches. Many college students go to Pensacola to sunbathe, go surfing and wind surfing. Thousands of college students enjoy spending holidays and summer months in the warm harbor of Pensacola. The Pensacola Naval Air Station is near Pensacola. Dan and Alisha saw a flight squadron known for its thrilling air shows. They are called Blue Angels.

Dan and Alisha walked on the long, coastal, pristine beaches. They went sailing in a sailboat in the harbor. The ocean sparkled and waves rippled to the shore. The view at sea was breathtaking. Dan and Alisha stayed at a seaside motel. They had a magnificent view of Pensacola Harbor.

The Strombergs traveled south along the Florida coast. They drove through Walton Beach to Panama City. The white sand beaches along the coast were picturesque. They stopped along the way to go swimming in the warm ocean. Finally they came to Port St. Joe where they stayed overnight. This seaport was interesting. They went to an amusement park there. Many amusements existed in this park. Dan and Alisha enjoyed browsing around.

The next day Dan and Alisha headed south to Apalachicola where they ate at an exotic, Mexican restaurant. The Mexican food was spicy, but very tasty. Dan and Alisha had cheese enchiladas, refried beans, rice and spinach tacos with spicy, cream sauce. They had flan for dessert and coffee. A Mexican waitress served them.

Later that day the Strombergs drove to Carrebelle along the coast. Carrebelle was a scenic resort where tourists came to enjoy the charm of this settlement. Dan and Alisha continued their journey down the coast. They went to Panacea, Medart and continued on their journey.

They came to Piney Grass Point which had beautiful pine trees and then to Pine Point with more pine trees. Horseshoe named after blacksmiths who made horseshoes for horses was another place to drive to. The Strombergs were becoming familiar with many places along the Florida Coast. Horseshoe Cove was a spectacular bay with a large cove worth viewing. Dan and Alisha rested there for several hours.

The Strombergs continued on to Demory Hill to Cedar Key named after magnificent cedar trees with red trunk bark and clustered leaves. The forest of cedar trees was very fragrant and healthy. Dan and Alisha were refreshed by their splendid aroma. They continued on to Yankeetown named after settlers from the East Coast of America. They came to Crystal Bay and saw Crystal River flowing majestically. They stopped here and had an afternoon picnic lunch of tuna sandwiches, potato salad, pickles and fresh oranges and herb tea.

Dan and Alisha drove on to Homossa near the West Florida Coast. They came to Chassahowitzka Bay which was another picturesque place. They drove on to Indian Bay named after the Florida Indians. Many Indians had settled in this area many years ago. They continued on to Port Richey where they stayed in a motel near the coast and enjoyed a magnificent sunset while they ate a fresh fish dinner with baked potatoes, a green salad with homemade, Indian cornbread and berry pie.

The next morning Dan and Alisha continued traveling to Tarpon Springs after breakfast. They came to Crystal Beach where they walked on a beautiful beach. They went swimming in the warm ocean to relax. Dan and Alisha continued on to Clearwater which was a larger town as they drove south along the Florida Coast. They ate at an Italian restaurant in Clearwater during lunchtime.

Then Dan and Alisha drove to Tampa, which was a large city. Tampa Bay is another popular beach site with many oceanside activities such as surfing, wind surfing, swimming and snorkeling. Dan and Alisha stayed in Tampa for several days and nights. They went surfing in Tampa Bay on rented surfboards. Then they went snorkeling in the ocean. They saw plankton, kelp and sea life in the ocean. Many tourists were vacationing in Tampa. Dan and Alisha went to a famous park with an African theme called Busch Gardens in Tampa. They saw African animals and plants and there were exciting rides.

The Strombergs continued southwest to St. Petersburg which is on the Central Coast of Florida. They noticed Spanish architecture and Spanish cathedrals in St. Petersburg. There were many palm and pine trees surrounding this city. Dan and Alisha enjoyed a Spanish environment in St. Petersburg.

Next, the Strombergs headed to Bradenton which was south of St. Petersburg. From Bradenton they went to Saratoga where they rested and had lunch. They came to Charlotte Harbor which was magnificent because of the beaches. They witnessed colorful sunsets. Dan and Alisha went swimming in the harbor and they sunbathed on the beach in Charlotte Harbor.

Dan and Alisha traveled south to St. James City which was named after St. James in the Bible. They continued to Naples. The beaches were very beautiful. They went swimming to cool off. They headed to Big Marco Bay to Marco. The rich, green scenery manifested a sense of peace and harmony. They stopped in Chakoloskee which was near Ten Thousand Islands which could be seen in the ocean in the harbor.

Dan and Alisha sailed to Ten Thousand Islands. There were palm trees and some pine trees on small islands. The remote beaches were deserted. They had a picnic lunch on one of the beaches. They explored the small islands. Sea birds nested and flew in flocks on these islands.

The next morning Dan and Alisha continued on to the famous Everglades. They took a motorboat and went into the Everglades through Evergreen National Park. They saw mangrove trees, bamboo reeds and swampy plants and green moss. There were a lot of alligators moving around. Mosquitoes pestered them. So they rubbed on insect repellant to ward off the mosquitoes.

Dan and Alisha observed roseate spoonbills feed on marine life in Everglades National Park. Fish eating birds called anhingas were flying around scooping down into the swampy Everglades for fish with their sharp beaks. When Dan and Alisha went hiking in the Everglades they saw large, green sea turtles walking in sand near the dense foliage. Turtles weighing hundreds of pounds can be spotted as well as water birds. Dan and Alisha observed Florida black panthers moving in Everglades National Park.

The Everglades in Southern Florida has 2,750 square miles of huge, swampy areas. Few people live in Everglades National Park. There are plenty of alligators, crocodiles, deer, turtles and water birds.

Dan and Alisha found out that Florida has no mountains. Florida is a peninsula in a tropical area in southern America. Florida is a Spanish word that means "full of flowers." The state flower is the orange blossom. The state bird is the mockingbird. The state marine mammal is the manatee. The state salt water mammal is the dolphin. Some other wildlife are bears, bobcats, foxes, beavers, otters, skunks, pelicans, storks, woodpeckers, cranes, herons, bald eagles, egrets and water turkeys. Fishing products are shrimp, lobsters, crabs, oysters, sponges, scallops, pompanos, red snappers, groupers and mullets.

Dan and Alisha drove across a long bridge from the southern tip of Florida to Key West, which is the warmest place in the U.S.A. The name key comes from cayo, Spanish for "small island." English speaking people changed cayo to key. There are hundreds of Florida Keys. About thirty of the main islands can be reached by car or on the Overseas Highway which connects many of the Florida Keys.

Dan and Alisha discovered that Key West was "a beguiling, eccentric, raffishingly charming end-of-the-road outpost." Dan and Alisha went to Little White House Museum which displayed historical events in the U.S.A. Downtown Key West had tin roofs, plantation shutters and clapboard sidings typifying Old Key West buildings.

The next day Dan and Alisha took a 90 minute, 14 mile narrated island tour. This gasoline powered open-air trolley is pulled by a tractor fancifully disguised as a miniature locomotive which leaves Mallory Square to Roosevelt Boulevard every half hour from 9:30 a.m. to 4:30 p.m. Later Dan and Alisha took the Old Town Trolley on a sightseeing trip.

Dan and Alisha went to the Audubon House and Tropical Gardens. They toured the Geiger family home. They toured the Heritage House Museum and Curry Mansion Inn. Key West's conch style buildings reflect carpenters who created them. They were built to deal with subtropical heat, humidity and stormy weather. Top-hinged shutters, ventilated attics, steep, galvanized, steel roofs for collecting rainwater was diverted to cisterns, columned, shade porches and piers instead of foundations to protect against flooding and rot exist in Key West.

The Old Key West Lighthouse had an eight-eight step, steel, spiral staircase inside the tower to its encircling catwalk. This 360 degree panorama is splendidly photogenic. This lighthouse tower stands out in Key West.

Ernest Hemingway built a two story house in 1931 in Key West. He lived in this high ceiling, elaborate home for 12 years. He continued to write books as well as to hunt, drink and travel. He wrote some of his best books entitled <u>Death In The Afternoon</u>, <u>The Green Hills Of Africa</u> and <u>To Have And Have Not</u>, an "enduring collection of extraordinary, short stories."

Ernest Hemingway furnished his home with ornate Venetian glass chandeliers. There is a small bookstore featuring Hemingway's works plus it was a souvenir shop. Hemingway wrote all his manuscripts in long hand. He hired other people to type his manuscripts.

Dan and Alicia toured Nancy Forrester's Secret Garden which

had orchids, ferns, bromeliads, cycads, flowering plants, vines and more than 150 species of palm trees. Nancy Forrester's garden is not really secret. Yet, tourists feel a sense of discovery as they walk through this garden. Dan and Alisha were enchanted with the many cultural activities in Key West.

Dan and Alisha drove back over the Overseas Highway to the southern tip of Florida. They continued their trip to Miami, one of the largest cities in Florida. They walked on South Beach, which is a very long beach. Many tourists were walking on this pristine, sandy beach. They sunbathed and went swimming in the warm ocean. Many skyscraper buildings and hotels have been built near one another along Miami Beach.

Tourists and other beach strollers had parties on South Beach and Miami Beach. Dan and Alisha ate at Mango's Tropical Café which had a Cuban setting. Latin dances were performed in this café. There are many bars and restaurants along the Miami beaches on the main, beachside street.

The night life in Miami is exciting. Bars and nightclubs are open until 2:00 a.m. each night. There are many singers and dancers who perform for many hours. Dan and Alisha stayed in a downtown, beachside hotel. They went to several, well known nightclubs to enjoy nightly entertainment. They drank several cocktails. They stayed up quite late in order to celebrate.

Dan and Alisha stayed in Miami for several days. The sunsets in Miami are heavenly. Bright, orangish-red sunsets reflect on the ocean for miles. Dan and Alisha went on a fishing boat. They caught several, saltwater anglers. They saw long necked cranes walking in the shallow, ocean water silhouetted against a brilliant sunset.

Dan and Alisha went in a glass bottom boat to see sea life in the deep ocean. They saw sharks, dolphins, manatee and plankton in the ocean. They were fascinated with the variety of sea creatures.

The Strombergs took an airflight to Orlando, Florida so they could go to Disney World. Their adventures at Disney World were extraordinary. They toured a Middle East section, an authentic, safari land and Chinese architectural setting. They even saw a duplicate setting of Venice in Italy. They ate exotic, Mediterranean food at a European, Mediterranean restaurant. They ate leg of lamb, rice pilaf and a medley of spicy, steamed vegetables. They had whole wheat homemade bread with asparagus soup. For dessert Dan and Alisha had chiffon cake with a creamy, berry sauce. It was all very sumptuous.

The Stromberg's flew back to Minneapolis, Minnesota after their three days, two nights adventures at Disney World, which was a special highlight during their vacation in Florida. They reminisced about their four weeks' vacation in Florida.

Staying In A Barn

Staying in a barn can be a challenging experience. A barn is not insulated. So a barn is generally drafty and cold especially at night. Barns are built to keep farm and ranch animals in. Hay and barley are stored there.

A barn is a rustic place for a person to live in. There is no fireplace or kitchen. A bathroom may not be available either. A person must adjust to the changing temperatures. A person must wear warm clothing during cold weather.

A healthy person can adjust better in a barn. An unhealthy person shouldn't live in a barn. He or she may come down with a cold. He or she may even get flu or bronchitis. Cold, damp air is not good to sleep in.

Barns usually do not have beds. A person usually would sleep in a hayloft or on hay spread out on the barn floor. There are no windows in a barn so it can get quite dark inside especially when the sun had gone over the horizon.

A person who sleeps in a dark barn at night is susceptible to crawling insects such as spiders, gnats, flies, mosquitoes and potato bugs, etc. Spider webs are woven and they usually exist in different locations in a barn. Black widows usually dwell in dark places in a barn. They crawl around in the barn. A person can get bit by black widows in a barn.

Flashlights and electric, generated lamps should be used if a person stays in a barn. A self generated heater should be used in a barn when it gets extremely cold. A Bunsen burner can be used to heat food and water. An ice bucket can be used to store cold drinks and perishable food such as fruit and vegetables.

Bedrolls and moveable beds can be put in a barn. Warm blankets should be use to cover over a person's bedroll. A person should bundle up in warm clothing before going to bed in cold, winter months.

There is no television or radios in barns. A person should bring books, magazines and newspapers to read while they stay in a barn. Reading is a relaxing form of entertainment.

Some barns are used for farm animals such as horses, cows and chickens. Charlotte's Web is a book about barn life. The author, E. B. White describes how barn animals behave in a barn. Charlotte was a spider. She observed dangers. She wove the word HELP in her web.

Wilma and Jared Arnoldson decided to hitchhike across America. They carried backpacks with them while they traveled by foot. They put their thumbs up to attract passing vehicles. They kept walking along a paved, two lane road.

Cars, trucks and vans passed by on the road. No one stopped to pick Wilma and Jared up. They continued to walk at the side of the road in the piercing sun. They walked for hours. Finally they decided to stop to rest in a nearby apple grove. They sat under a big, apple tree after picking ripe, red apples off the ground. They ate the raw apples they collected. They were refreshed from eating the fresh apples.

Wilma and Jared rested under the shade of a large, leafy, apple tree for a period of time. Then they walked out of the apple orchard. They came to an old, deserted barn in a field of weeds.

The barn had openings in the walls. The roof was in shambles with more open rafters. Wilma and Jared walked into the barn. They saw loose lumber on the floor in the barn. Wilma found a section in the back of the barn.

Wilma and Jared decided to stay in the old barn overnight. They laid their backpacks down in a corner. They brushed the floor and unrolled their bedrolls. Wilma took a flashlight out of her backpack to turn on when it got dark. She also took out some wrapped tuna sandwiches and can of cola to eat for lunch. She sat on her bedroll and unwrapped her sandwich. She began eating her tuna sandwich. Then she sipped her cola.

Suddenly Wilma saw a rat scurrying across the barn, she reacted with fear and anxiety. The rat came over closer to Wilma. It sniffed the tuna sandwich in the air. Jared rushed over with a long stick and scared the rat away. He came over to Wilma to comfort her.

Jared said, "That rat must be hungry! It won't bother you now." Wilma made a sigh of relief. She replied, "I hope the rat doesn't come back! We better be careful when it gets dark!" Jared looked concerned. He answered, "I will watch carefully for rats." Wilma continued to eat her sandwich and sip her cola.

The sunlight blazed into the open cracks in the old, dilapidated walls. The warmth of the sun rays was comforting. It would get colder as the day went on. Jared had unrolled his bedroll and laid it on the hard, wood floor near Wilma's bedroll. He also unpacked his backpack. He took out a salami-tomato sandwich. He sat on his bedroll and began eating his sandwich. He drank a can of root beer.

Wilma and Jared were not sure what would happen while they stayed in the rustic, old barn. After they were done eating their lunch they decided to improve the barn. They straightened out loose boards.

They took nails out of old boards. Jared took a solid stone to use as a hammer. He began nailing old lumber over the cracks and openings in the barn walls.

Wilma found another solid rock to use as a hammer. She decided to nail some loose boards in cracks and openings in some barn walls. Wilma and Jared sealed as many openings that they could so that the barn was more insulated. Jared climbed up on the barn roof with more pieces of wood.

Once the old barn was repaired Wilma and Jared rested to recuperate from working so hard to restore the barn. Wilma and Jared decided to wander around outside. They walked in a nearby meadow where there were some wild dandelions, poppies and lupines. There were wild berries growing on berry bushes. They picked the wild berries and placed them in a bag.

Jared and Wilma noticed that the sun was going down in the West. They walked back across the meadow and field of weeds back to the barn. They went into the repaired barn. They ate wild berries for dinner. There was no television or radio to enjoy.

Wilma had a paperback novel in her backpack which she found in a bookstore for $14.95. She took the paperback book out of her travel bag to read. It was entitled, <u>Westward Pursuit</u> by Cecelia Frances Page. Jared took out a paperback book entitled <u>Opportune Times</u> written by Cecelia Frances Page to read. Both novels were purchased at the Halcyon Gift Store in Halcyon, California.

The Arnoldsons read for several hours by flashlight. Then they got into their bedrolls and tried to go to sleep. They heard noises outside. An owl was hooting repeatedly. They heard wild animals scratching outside on the barn walls. Then they heard a wolf howling in the distance. It was difficult to fall asleep.

Finally at about midnight Wilma and Jared fell asleep. Around 2:00 a.m. some rats came into the barn through some unseen cracks in the barn walls. The rats ran around the inside of the old barn. Several rats came over to Wilma's bedroll. They crawled on her bedroll and sniffed around.

Wilma woke up when she felt the rats crawling near her face. She saw the rats staring at her. She screamed because she was frightened. Jared woke up. He saw the rats. He got up and took a long stick. He pointed the stick at them to shoo them away. There were six rats running around the barn. Jared opened the barn door and the rats ran outside.

Meanwhile, Wilma was shaking with fright. She was afraid to fall asleep again. She turned on her flashlight. Jared said, "At least we weren't bitten by those rats!" Wilma replied, "I want to leave tomorrow morning. I won't sleep in this barn another night!" Jared responded, "I understand how you feel."

Wilma and Jared tried to rest but they didn't go to sleep. They hoped no more rats would come into the barn. The next morning after eating berries and some bread they packed in their backpacks they left the old barn.

The Arnoldsons continued their journey around America. They hoped they would be able to hitchhike so they could travel for miles across the countryside. They avoided staying in deserted, old barns.

TWELVE

SPIRULINA PRODUCTS

Spirulina was discovered in the 1960s. Green, algae nutrients were combined to produce spirulina. The nutrients in spirulina are rich in chlorophyll, iron and algae.

Spirulina was produced so that many people can receive the best nutrients possible. There is protein in the algae. Spirulina is produced in capsules and put in packaged bottles.

Spirulina has made a difference in improving different people's lives. It is sold in many health food stores and online through the Internet. The cost of spirulina is generally reasonable. Spirulina has become well known in forty years. It is a valuable, healthful product many people use to stay healthy.

Spirulina can be mail-ordered to customers. It has been proven that spirulina boosts a person's vitality and immune system. Spirulina is a worthwhile discovery in promoting the health of many people. Keep spirulina in a cool, dry place so it will be preserved longer. Order more spirulina in time.

Supplements can be added to spirulina such as gamma linclenic acid (GLA), protein, Vitamin A, Thiamine B-1, Roboflavin B-2, B-12, calcium and iron. Spirulina is grown in Hawaii. You can purchase spirulina tablets at a vitamin and herb store and at regular, health stores. Spirulina tablets are sold in 100 or 200 tablets in each bottle.

Spirulina was discovered in the ocean. Green algae and plankton are found in the oceans of the world. It has become a truly, revolutionary discovery. Spirulina will be around for a long time. More and more people are benefiting when they take spirulina tablets. They are healthier and they generally live longer.

THIRTEEN

BUILDING A HOUSE

Building a substantial, well-built home takes planning. A good architectural draft helps the house last longer because it is more durable. There are houses with one bedroom, two bedrooms, three bedrooms and even four bedrooms. There are one story to four story homes.

Some houses are made with cement. Other homes are made with wood and bricks. Some homes are built in tracts. Other homes are built on platforms. All homes are required to have cement foundations according to building codes and requirements.

Every home has windows put in the outside walls to bring in light and fresh air, sunlight can come into windows. Windows provide the opportunity for people so see views in their surroundings.

A well built house has solid wall frames that are sound proofed and durable. Electric wiring is installed in the framework in the walls. State code, electric wiring must be used in each house.

Once electric wiring is installed the wall frames are covered with wall coverings. The floors are covered with cut, nailed lumber. Then carpets and linoleum are carefully placed on the floors throughout the house.

There are different kinds of homes which are appealing. A plantation home is usually made with thick, wide, brick walls. Bricks are put together one by one with cement mortar. The walls are long and high. Each room is very large. A plantation is built in two or three stories. Clay tile roofs are placed together with mortar on the large roof. Spacious rooms are decorated with elegant furniture. Canopy beds are put in the big bedrooms. Fancy curtains are placed on the windows.

Magnificent carpeting covers many floors in the plantation homes. Many plantation homes have hanging chandeliers in the living room, parlor room and dining room. The outdoor grounds are arranged with beautiful gardens.

Mansion homes with majestic columns and large, stately exteriors are built in southern states. The rooms are very large with high ceilings. Mansion homes have many bedrooms and bathrooms. Elegant furniture is imported from France and England. French curtains are placed over large, framed windows.

Modern tract homes with painted roofs, with nailed on shingles are commonly built in many communities. Victorian styled three story homes have gables and fancy exteriors. Adjoining apartments are built to provide compartments for many people.

All homes, mansions, plantation homes and apartments are inspected by building inspectors and they must be approved by them before they are completed, sold and lived in. The building inspectors carefully examine how each house and apartment was built. Safety codes and building standards must be passed in each building before anyone can dwell in them.

Building a house takes knowledge and specific, building plans. Specific, building materials must be purchased. Building foundations and plumbing methods as well as electrical facilities have to pass inspection. Houses must be safely built before they pass building codes. Carpenters, electricians, plumbers, landscapers and architects all help to contribute to the building of a house.

FOURTEEN

LIVING IN THE
17ᵀᴴ THROUGH 21ˢᵀ CENTURIES

During the 17th Century people from Europe came to America as pilgrims and pioneers. The 17th Century was a time of migration, change and settlement of new lands.

Pilgrims fled from Europe to escape from religious bigotry, severe poverty and lack of personal freedom. The pilgrims had to find ways to survive in the new wilderness. They built settlements to live in. They had to gather food. They hunted for game and planted vegetables and fruits. They made their own clothes, shoes and did all household and farming chores.

In the 17th Century there were many superstitions and religious persecutions. Many people were punished and put to death unfairly. Many pilgrims and settlers had to endure many hardships, diseases and early death. Pioneers who survived developed the thirteen colonies.

Pioneers continued to travel West to settle in the territories in the Midwest and far Western regions. America began to expand and grow. More and more people came to America to settle down and live permanently. They developed farms, ranches and towns. They continued to populate America.

During the 18th Century Napoleon tried to take over Europe. The English government went to war against France. Eventually, Napoleon was defeated. He was exiled to an island after the War. Mussolini became a dictator in Italy.

Queen Elizabeth the First sent explorers to discover the New World. Great Britain became a strong leader around the world. England acquired many territories and colonies around the world. Explorers drew maps of different locations in the world. Many English settlers traveled to English colonies and territories to live and establish settlements.

Once many places had been developed and expanded life continued with more freedom and prosperity. During the 18th Century cultural pursuits existed. Shakespeare's plays became known in England. Artists created paintings of landscapes, seascapes and portraits of different people. Oil paintings were popular.

During the 19th Century trains were built and used. People could travel better and farther on trains. More inventions such as cameras, cars, trolleys, cable cars, farm machinery, Morse Code, telegraphs, typewriters and electricity were invented. These many inventions made it easier to live.

Ships without sails and submarines were invented in the 19th Century. People could navigate across oceans faster with more safety. They could travel farther more comfortably. Passenger ships were available for tourists to travel abroad.

The 19th and 20th Centuries were opportunities for technology to develop. Office machines were created in the 20th Century. Eventually computers were invented. Refrigeration, modern, electric and gas stoves were invented. Microwave ovens and toasters were created so that cooking was faster and easier.

Life in the 20th Century was much easier. Many household inventions such as vacuum cleaners, irons, heaters, refrigerators, electric shavers, toothbrushes and massaging devices, comfortable waterbeds and other modern beds, lamps and central lighting and heating were created. Spas and saunas as well as swimming pools were invented and widely used.

During the 19th Century Theosophy was introduced by Madame Helena Blavatsky. She traveled to England, India and to New York City. She wrote a variety of theosophical books and pamphlets to enlighten people. During the 18th, 19th and early 20th Centuries European and American literature became well known and read in public, private schools and colleges.

Hollywood movies began in the early 20th Century. Many black and white and colored films have been created. Television and radios are more inventions to bring entertainment readily into everyone's home. We can listen to a variety of music and news. There are many programs on television such as travelogues, historical documentaries, scientific topics, movies, news, music and soap operas, etc.

In the 21st Century computers are even more sophisticated. Larger television screens are used in people's homes and stereophonic music is popular in many homes. There are many luxuries in most homes. Many household inventions make life much easier and more enjoyable.

More students are attending college. They have an opportunity to receive a good education. They have better opportunities to have better jobs and occupations. People can travel all over the world. People use computers to write e-mail messages. Computers are used to process school reports and other papers. Computers are used for doing research. We have an opportunity to learn many things during the 21st Century.

FIFTEEN

HATS AND BONNETS

During cold or hot weather and rainy weather people usually wear hats. Bonnets were worn by women in the 17th and 18th Centuries. Hats protect a person's head and face from sun and wind. Rain hats keep rain off of a person's face.

Hats of all types have been made for thousands of years. Hats are made in many shapes and fabrics. There are many colors. There are corduroy hats, Irish hats, sombreros, hats made with caps, straw hats, dressy rimmed hats and more.

Hats are worn for various occasions. A top hat is worn at special celebrations. They are worn by men in England in high society. Royalty men sometimes wear top hats. Top hats have been worn in Broadway performances and variety shows. They are worn in Vaudeville shows.

Hats are worn for appearances. They look attractive on men. Women look attractive when they wear different well made hats. Women wear many shapes when they wear hats. Some wear veils on their hats. They wear hats for special occasions. Generally women may wear a formal hat to a wedding and to a funeral, a reception and to other, formal occasions. Women wear hats to church on Sunday mornings. They dress up and then decide to wear fancy hats.

Bonnets were made long ago in Europe. Bonnets cover a woman's ears and their foreheads and the sides of their face. Bonnets were worn in early America by many women. Women who lived in the Midwest and farther West wore bonnets to protect their heads.

Many women know how to sew bonnets to wear every day. Bonnets are made with cotton cloth and with different colors. Women dyed cotton cloth different colors such as yellow, blue and green. Bonnets are useful and can be attractive on women. We seldom see bonnets in the 21st Century because they are no longer worn by women.

Hats and bonnets have their place in the world. Hats are still worn. Many hats are popular.

---------------------------- SIXTEEN ----------------------------

DISCUSSIONS

There are many discussion groups. Discussions take place in hobby groups, after church meetings, in college classrooms, at PTA meetings, at community meetings and at interest clubs, etc.

Stimulating discussions can take place if there are worthwhile topics and issues to talk about. For instance, a discussion group leader can lead groups in stimulating discussions by asking thinking questions to encourage discussion group members to respond with answers to questions.

At The Temple of the People in Halcyon, California a discussions group meets every Friday afternoon at the University Center. Everyone has the opportunity to respond and share their comments and ideas about Temple lessons. Each Temple lesson is a different subject. Members of the group have different ideas and interpretations about different concepts and knowledge presented in each lesson.

There are three volumes entitled The Temple Teachings, Volume I, II, and III. There are hundreds of lessons to study. Members of the discussion group have expanded their awareness about reincarnation, karma (cause and effect), centralization, law of polarity, electromagnetism, balance and equilibrium, matter, force and consciousness and many, more subjects.

People who participate in discussion groups usually learn to listen to others and they contribute good ideas in the discussion. Members of the group can learn from each other. Different viewpoints are voiced by different participants about the same question. Individuals see things in a different way. This adds to the enrichment of each discussion.

SEVENTEEN

HORSE AND BUGGY DAYS

During the 16th Century to the early 20th Century people traveled by horse and buggy. Horses were tied to the buggy which they pulled for many miles. One or two horses were generally used to pull a buggy.

Horses needed to be carefully washed and groomed. They were fed hay and barley. They drank water in a bucket or trough. Horses ate grass in fields and meadows. Horses were kept in barns or stables when they were not being used to pull buggies.

Some horses were stronger than other horses. They had to be well cared for in order to remain healthy. When the weather became colder especially in the late Fall and Winter months horses kept warmer when they wore a warm cover over their bodies. They wore a muffler over their face to shield them from severely, cold weather.

Horses respond better if they are treated pleasantly. They enjoy eating apples, sugar cubes and carrots. Some horse owners knew how to communicate effectively to their horses. They knew how to strap their horses properly to the buggies. Horses respond much better if they are treated gently with respect.

Children who show respect to their horses and give them attention generally help their horses live longer. Horses like to be petted and stroked. Horses respond to affection and a warm, loving touch.

Buggies needed to be properly cared for. Owners used to clean their buggies so that people who rode in them were comfortable as well as safe to ride in. Strong straps were necessary to use to maintain safety.

Well cared for horses were able to ride farther and better. They needed to rest at places where they stopped. Horses should have their own space to rest. They should have their hooves checked regularly in order to protect their horses from painful accidents.

Horse and buggy days are over today because people drive cars, vans and trucks. They also ride bicycles for transportation. However, movies are made showing the use of horse and buggies in different eras in history.

We are reminded of earlier times when cars, vans, trucks and bicycles were not available. Horses and buggies will have a special memory in people's minds as a bygone experience.

Some buggies were fancier than other buggies. Fancy buggies had frills on them. Other buggies did not have a protective cover above the seats. Some buggies were painted black while other buggies were painted white or red.

Horses and buggies are displayed at Disneyland, the County Fair and ranches. They have a special place in history. Amish people still ride in horse and buggies in their Amish villages because they believe in living in an old-fashioned manner. They do not believe in modern methods of transportation.

EIGHTEEN

WAREHOUSE INFORMATION

Most supermarkets and well known stores have warehouses to store their commercial goods and produce. Canned goods are stocked in shelves and are priced by stock clerks. Many necessary store supplies and products are kept in warehouses.

Warehouses are usually very large so that many things can be stored and used when necessary. Warehouses are usually guarded by security guards to protect store merchandise. Otherwise store merchandise can be stolen. It would be very costly to lose store merchandise.

Merchandise was shipped from far away places to specific warehouses. Stock clerks must check the incoming merchandise and sign for it. Inventory lists are kept for all merchandise. The inventory list is carefully checked to be sure all merchandise is properly stocked and stored in warehouses.

There are many types of merchandise stored in warehouses. Even clothes and furs may be stored in shelves and on racks in warehouses. Furs must be carefully guarded because they generally are very expensive. Many clothes are expensive such as wedding dresses, dressy gowns, quality suits for men and women and expensive shoes. Jewelry is generally expensive. It must be carefully stored and guarded so it won't be stolen.

Warehouses are necessary to collect and preserve a wide variety of merchandise. Without warehouses large stores and supermarkets wouldn't be able to stay open. Store goods must be available to replace merchandise that has been sold. People want merchandise as soon as possible. The requested merchandise can be sent for at the warehouses much more quickly because the warehouse is usually nearby.

It can take much longer to receive merchandise that has been shipped to the warehouse. It is convenient to go to the warehouse to purchase requested items.

Some merchandise is kept in boxes. The boxes of merchandise are stored in warehouses. They are opened when needed in the stores.

Warehouses need to be kept cool and dry to preserve all of the merchandise. The temperature must be regulated and controlled to protect the supplies and goods.

Nineteen

ROLES OF MAYORS

Mayors are elected to become administrators in towns and cities. A mayor helps to establish policies and laws to improve local government. A mayor selects a town or city council that works with the mayor to make changes in government policies and procedures.

Mayors usually have a lot of influence because they make important decisions about issues of concern in the community. For instance, economic issues are discussed. How tax money is distributed to pay for roads, public buildings, school supplies and educational goals, hospital costs and many other needs is important.

Mayors delegate responsibilities to their councilmen and women. These councilmen and women help develop new laws, propositions and policies. Roads need to be improved in towns and cities. Public buildings need to be repaired and restored. New buildings need to be built at different schools, etc.

When there are severe earthquakes and floods emergency, tax money is used to repair damages caused by severe weather and cataclysms.

Whole towns and sections of cities may have to be restored. It takes emergency, tax monies to restore the damages.

Mayors and their councilmen and women must work closely together to make wise decisions to protect the towns and cities step by step. They can promote positive changes to improve the towns and cities they are administrators in.

A mayor may eventually become a governor. A mayor may become a state representative or a state senator or congressman or congresswoman. The roles of mayors are of significance in promoting worthwhile changes in towns and cities.

TWENTY

REFRIGERATOR ADVANTAGES

Refrigerators were invented in the early 20th Century. They were used to keep food cold to preserve it. Milk, cheese, meat, cooked vegetables and fruit, butter, eggs, jelly preserves and leftovers, etc., are kept in refrigerators to preserve these foods.

Without refrigeration food would spoil rapidly. When food is kept cold it lasts much longer. Ice cream and sherbet stays solid and cold in a freezer which is stored in the upper part of a refrigerator.

Cut cake, pies, puddings and Jell-o is kept in a refrigerator. These desserts last much longer. Restaurant food is kept in refrigerators. Salads, sliced meats for sandwiches, cut, raw vegetables and fruit, tapioca pudding, applesauce and more food are refrigerated to be served to customers.

Delicatessens preserve sliced meat and cheese as well as lettuce, tomatoes and pickles, potato salad, carrot salad, coleslaw, cold drinks, cheesecake, apple pie, peach and berry pie are kept in refrigerators to keep these foods preserved.

Delicatessens are in a section in supermarkets. People can purchase sandwiches, a variety of salads, desserts and a variety of cold drinks which are available. People, who are in a hurry on their lunch break, go to delicatessens to order food to go. Refrigeration makes it possible for preserved food to be served to many people.

The use of refrigeration makes it possible to serve more food which may be a day or two old. Food which is cold can be reheated again to serve. Food is not wasted when it can be preserved longer.

Frozen food even lasts much longer because the colder food is the longer it is preserved. Once food is unthawed it must be cooked and eaten. Ice cream and sherbet lasts a long time. It can be eaten readily once it is take out of the freezer to be served. Frozen foods in packages, ice cream, sherbet and meat are kept in freezers. Separate, larger freezers are used to store more frozen food.

Food can be transported for many miles because of refrigeration. Refrigeration is the best way to preserve perishable food in trucks. It may take several days to a week to deliver food across the country. It must be kept cold to preserve it while the truck driver travels many miles to deliver the food. Again, refrigeration makes it possible to preserve the food to be delivered to its destination.

TWENTY-ONE

WORTHWHILE AMBITIONS

There are many ambitions to pursue in the world. People who are ambitious usually have specific goals and purposes. They seek certain pursuits in their lives. Ambitious people usually accomplish their goals and desires. They are determined to achieve their objectives and to be successful in their ambitions.

Joseph Ladderman developed goals. He wanted to become a successful businessman. He went to college to study Business Administration. He completed all business courses in college to receive a B.S. in Business Administration.

Once Joseph Ladderman received his B. S. in Business he applied for business positions in Los Angeles, California. He had attended Santa Barbara Business College in Santa Maria, California. He had earned an A average in Business Administration.

Joseph went to twenty interviews before he was employed. He had a well organized resume with descriptions of his previous experiences in business. He had worked as a business clerk at a business firm in Santa Maria as a word processor. He also worked at a local newspaper as a bookkeeper. Joseph listed his address, home phone number, specific office skills such as computer experience, typing, filing and bookkeeping background.

Joseph began working as a business consultant for a local firm in the business section of Santa Barbara, California. He was assigned to the advertising department. It was Joseph's responsibility to help create ads for the business firm.

The business firm produced and sold cosmetic products. Facial creams, lipsticks, eyebrow pencils and eye liners were produced at this company. Joseph was expected to develop convincing, cosmetic commercials for television and newspaper advertising. He had to develop camera footage showing each cosmetic product.

Joseph worked with business partners in the advertising department. Each partner helped to produce dynamic advertising. The Cosmetic Business firm depended on advertising to sell the cosmetics.

Joseph managed to develop a variety of dynamic advertisements. He was very successful in the advertising department because his advertisements were circulated. Many people found out about the cosmetic products. Many cosmetics were sold. The business firm accumulated enough money to remain successful for many years.

Joseph worked hard for many years at the Santa Maria Cosmetic Firm. He eventually became a top, business executive. He coordinated the different, business departments. He was very ambitious. So he was a successful business executive. He received a top salary.

Joseph bought a $1.5 million dollar three story home with ten acres. He had beautiful gardens and a swimming pool and tennis court. Chandeliers were hanging in the living room. The house was covered with wall to wall carpeting and linoleum. Joseph was able to enjoy many household luxuries in his beautiful, spacious home. His ambition to become a businessman paid off.

Melissa Jennings grew up in a large family of twelve children in a poverty-stricken environment. She was the oldest child and she had many responsibilities in her parents' household. Melissa decided that she would break away from poverty some day. She planned to improve herself by doing well in school.

Education was Melissa's way of improving herself. She studied hard in school and earned above average grades. She was conscientious and became ambitious. She decided to pursue a different life than her parents. She wanted a better life with more opportunities than her parents.

Melissa finished high school with above average grades. She had to work to help support her parents, brothers and sisters. She worked as a waitress. She saved her wages and tips to give to her parents for five years. When she was twenty-three years old she began to realize that she didn't want to be a waitress for the rest of her life.

Melissa decided to save money to go to college. She still lived in her parents' home. She began to save 50% of her wages and all of her tips. She enrolled at a nearby junior college. She completed two years of general education. She earned a B average. She then signed up for a scholarship. She was given $10,000.00. She also signed up for a loan of $50,000.00.

A university was ten miles away. Melissa went on a public bus to this university to continue upper division courses. She decided to major in Home Economics. She had learned to sew and knit while she was growing up. She also knew how to cook well. She did a lot of cooking to help her mother prepare meals because she was the oldest child.

Melissa earned high grades in Home Economics. She worked hard and studied carefully in order to complete all her college courses in order to succeed in college. Within three years she completed her major in Home Economics. She also received a certificate in teaching and a B. A. in Home Economics.

Melissa Jennings was qualified to teach high school Home

Economics. She student taught at a high school near the university where she went to college. Melissa was able to get a teaching position in the same city where she grew up. She taught Home Economics to freshmen, sophomores, juniors and seniors. She became a popular teacher.

Melissa Jennings taught her high school students to cook and sew. Many students learned to cook and sew well. They enjoyed putting ingredients together when they cooked different recipes. Learning to knit was a challenge for many students. Melissa was patient with her students.

Ms. Jennings continued to teach Home Economics for years. She was a very successful teacher. She was well liked and respected. She knew the value of receiving an education. Melissa was ambitious so she was able to pursue her goals and ambition to become a teacher.

Twenty-Two

Cactus and Rock Gardens

Cactus plants grow in dry and sandy soil. Cactus plants absorb moisture and retain the moisture. Cactus plants are succulent. Succulent plants can live in dry and hot places.

Cactus plants produce cactus fruit which is delicious. Cactus fruit is useful in hot and dry deserts. Some cactus plants grow very high in Arizona, Nevada and New Mexico. Other cacti have sharp thorns and thick clusters of shapely leaves.

Cactus gardens exist in different locations in the world. A beautiful cactus garden exists between Morro Bay and Cambria in California. There are many cacti growing at the cactus garden. This in an unusual place where visitors can enjoy a wide variety of cacti plants planted in a special manner.

Rock gardens are unusual to look at. Rocks can be placed in very artistic patterns and designs. They can be painted on. They look colorful when they are painted with vivid colors.

Rocks are scenic when they are arranged especially for artistic reasons. Pebbles and smaller rocks are put in front yards in place of grass. Rocks keep weeds away from front and back yards. They are easy to use around the exterior of one's home.

The cactus garden near Cambria is one of a few cactus gardens with such a wide variety of cactus plants in San Luis Obispo County. People come far and wide to see this spectacular, cactus display in a garden setting. They take photographs of the cactus and their photographs can be shown at home and to friends and relatives. Photos can be displayed on bulletin boards and walls.

It is easy to grow a cactus garden because cactus plants require little water. They grow easily and continue to spread out in gardens and deserts.

TWENTY-THREE

KALEIDOSCOPES

Kaleidoscopes are very creative designs inside a sliding cylinder container. Many geometric designs can be created as a person turns the cylinder. Every geometric design is unique. Many designs can be seen and there are no repeated designs as the cylinder is slid clockwise slowly.

Kaleidoscopes were created several hundred years ago. Kaleidoscopes were sold at County Fairs and Carnivals. Many people were intrigued with these creative designs and unusual patterns of vivid colors.

Vivid purple, green, gold, red, pink, orange, blue and white are in the geometric designs that keep moving. Kaleidoscopes can be purchased at emporiums and gift shops. Kaleidoscopes fascinate children and adults.

Kaleidoscopes vary in prices. Large ones are more expensive. Small kaleidoscopes are less expensive. They are stored in shelves, drawers and glass cases.

Kaleidoscopes make wonderful gifts and birthday presents for many age groups. It is easy to wrap kaleidoscopes in boxes with colorful wrapping paper. Many people are pleased to receive kaleidoscopes.

Import and export shops import and export kaleidoscopes overseas. Kaleidoscopes are considered to be valuable and unusual because of their geometric designs.

TWENTY-FOUR

VIDEO SELECTIONS

Videos are very popular today. Videos are played on VCRs and DVDs. Many movies and films have been put on videos. People are able to rent out videos in video stores such as Blockbuster, Videos For Rent, Warehouse Videos, Borders' Videos and many more.

There are many types of videos available at video stores. Different types of videos are Adventure, Science Fiction, Romance, Travelogues, Mysteries, Family Life, Nature, Sea Life and more topics. Some videos have been produced in the 1970s on.

Videos are kept in plastic cases and labeled. They can easily be purchased and stored in shelves and cupboards. Some favorite videos are The King And I, The Sound Of Music, Oklahoma, West Side Story, My Fair Lady, Brigadoon, Cactus Flower, Barefoot In The Park, The Big Country, Giant, National Velvet and many more films which have been produced into videos.

The production of videos has made it possible for everyone to enjoy many films produced over a period of eighty years. The public has access to thousands of videos. As a result many people can learn many things about movies, travelogues and documentaries about history, religion, science, politics, education and many more topics.

The magic of videos provides the people around the world quality entertainment and knowledge of films and movies. Movies from 1925 through 2009 are now available as videos. People can rent and even purchase videos readily to review and to enjoy.

Videos are played in the classrooms, at community events, at church meetings, at special occasions and in people's homes. Television with VCRs attached to televisions are used to play videos whenever a person desires to select a video to watch.

───────── Twenty-Five ─────────

Composing Music

To become a composer of music takes understanding and knowledge about reading and recognizing music notes on the piano, guitar, violin and other musical instruments. The notes are different on each instrument.

Piano compositions are written in the treble and bass clef. More notes are written in both clefs. The melody is usually in the treble clef. The bass clef is usually the accompaniment which is in harmony with the melody.

Wolfgang Amadeus Mozart began composing piano pieces at the age of five years old. He was a child prodigy. He was capable of composing sophisticated melodies and background accompaniments to add to the embellishment of each composition.

It takes a creative imagination and different ways to create a worthwhile piano composition. The melody should be in the same major or minor key so the melody will be in harmony. Major keys are in sharps. Minor keys are in flats. Beautiful melodies can be composed.

George Frideric Handel wrote <u>The Messiah</u> which is one of the most beautiful religious, vocal music in four part harmony. The Messiah is one of the longest, religious choir music. The Messiah is sung at Easter time and even at Christmas time. It is inspirational music. Handel spent time writing each vocal part. Each vocal part is in harmony with the other vocal parts. An organ or piano is played as accompaniment background to The Messiah.

Frederic Chopin began composing magnificent, piano compositions after he learned to play the piano. His concertos, etudes and sonatas are superb and of the highest quality. Chopin is one of the greatest composers of piano music. His piano solos are appreciated around the world over a period of centuries because of his mastery in composing first class, piano music.

So, learn to play a musical instrument. Who knows? You may learn to compose wonderful, original compositions.

TWENTY-SIX

BEDSPREADS AND QUILTS

Bedspreads are covered over beds. They add color and designs to beds. Pillows are tucked inside the bedspread to add an attractive appearance to double and single beds. Colorful pillows can be placed on beds and couches.

Some bedspreads are very bright with vivid colors. Other bedspreads are one straight color. Some bedspreads are white, or blue or black and even red. Bedspreads protect the blankets, sheets and pillows underneath the bedspread.

Bedrooms look much more attractive when beds are covered properly with interesting bedspreads. Curtains should match the bedspreads and carpets. Each bedroom should be decorated differently to make a home more interesting.

Quilts are handmade or machine made with wool or patches of contrasting cotton cloth. The patches are sewn together to make a bed covering. Quilts are authentic and created to be put over couches as well as beds and even on rocking chairs and recliner chairs. Quilts have been sewn for hundreds of years. They are unique and different.

Pioneer women in America organized quilting bees. Pioneer women gathered together to make quilts while they socialized. This gave them the opportunity to enjoy visiting and catching up about local news and happenings while they were busy sewing patches of cloth to make quilts. They had collected square patches to use.

Quilts are not handmade anymore. This old fashioned custom, which once was practiced, is gone. Quilts are made with machines in sewing factories.

TWENTY-SEVEN

ATTRACTIVE HAIRSTYLES

Attractive hairstyles help women and men look better. Some women wear very short hairstyles. Other women have long hair. Women with long hairdos are able to wear many, different hairstyles.

Women with long hairstyles look quite attractive with rolled curls on their heads and long, dangling curls. Long, straight hair evenly cut on the ends is attractive. Hair is parted on the side or fluffed up with body. Curls carefully produce softness and fullness around a woman's face.

Short hairstyles are easy to style with hair blowers. Women wash their hair and blow dry their hair in stylish shapes to help them look attractive. They curve their hair in a certain manner to make their faces look good.

Hair is cut in a special manner in the back. The hair is tapered carefully so it is easy to comb. There are no loose, out-of-place hairs. Short hair can be fluffed, laced and feathered to create specific, modern hairstyles. Hairspray may be used to hold hair into the proper styles.

Women experiment with different hair colors to add flair and more color to their hair. Hair color can add attractiveness to women who normally would have gray hair. They look younger with youthful, looking hair.

Men wear attractive hair cuts. Their hair is tapered and shaped in a manner to enhance their faces. Men also have their hair colored blonde, brown, red and black. They look younger when they have no bald spots in their hair.

Men use hair medication on their scalps to grow hair back where there are bald spots. Filled-in hair usually looks better than bald spots. Gray is taken out of men's hair to help them look younger.

Men have their hair tapered along the sides and back to look more distinguished. Full waves of hair are kept on top of men's heads. Men can wear a variety of short hairstyles. Barbers know how to use electric razors to taper hair around the sides and back of men's heads. Men look attractive with neatly cut hairstyles.

Men and women look attractive with creative hairdos. Some men and women experiment and have their hair tinted orange, pink, green or blue. They want to look unusually different so they will be noticed. However, these bizarre, unnatural hair colors are not really attractive.

Some men wear Mohawk hairstyles. Mohawk hairstyles are unconventional. Conventional men usually do not wear Mohawk or other American Indian hairdos.

Some women have their hair styled once a week in beauty parlors in order to wear attractive hairstyles. Men have their hair cut usually once a month to maintain attractive, neat hairdos.

TWENTY-EIGHT

LIFE IN HALCYON

Life in Halcyon, California is a special experience. There are approximately one hundred people living there. Most of the people know each other quite well. Around fifty Halcyonites behave like sisters and brothers because of their religious experiences at The Temple of the People in Halcyon.

There are community potlucks in the Hiawatha Lodge during holidays such as Christmas Day, Thanksgiving Day, Veterans Day and Easter Sunday. Birthday parties, wedding receptions and special presentations take place regularly in the Hiawatha Lodge. It is a place to gather together to share memorable occasions.

When a crisis takes place such as a sudden illness, damage of cars, a fire outside, etc, neighbors usually come to the rescue to help the neighbor who is having the crisis. Examples of neighborly help are as follows. Someone was riding his bicycle in Halcyon on one of the Halcyon streets. He suddenly fell off his bicycle and he broke his left ankle. He was unable to get up. He lay on the side of the street helpless. Someone in Halcyon was driving by and saw this person lying on the ground looking helpless. He stopped his car and went to him. He managed to assist this injured person to the nearby hospital to the Emergency Ward. He was cared for in the hospital.

Halcyonites came to the hospital to visit with the injured person who lived in Halcyon. They brought cards, flowers and food to him to cheer him up. Eventually he was released from the hospital. The same neighbor picked him up to bring him to his home. Everyone was concerned how he was recovering. They cared about what happened to him.

Temple members pray for other Halcyonites. There is a noon service where healing prayers are repeated every day. There are two weekly meetings where Temple members and visitors sit in a circle to discuss Temple lessons. The discussions are deep and profound.

Homes in Halcyon are spread apart with trees, grass and plenty of space and privacy. There are eucalyptus groves around the village of Halcyon which are fragrant. The aroma of eucalyptus leaves and bark emanate healthy air for Halcyonites to breathe.

Blue jays, robins, quails, sparrows, doves and meadowlarks chirp in the woods and in different trees around town. Many colorful birds fly around and they dwell in gardens to eat grass and nectar from flowers in the gardens around Halcyon. Raccoons, rabbits and dogs roam around Halcyon especially at night. They scratch their paws on the walls of different homes during the night time. These creatures are seeking shelter under the eaves of homes.

Halcyon is a beautiful place with no crime. The people live in peace and harmony. Kids have come into Halcyon to throw rocks at windows in The Temple building. They were finally caught. These out-of-town mischief makers were counseled and warned about their vandalism. The church leaders forgave them and gave them another chance. They never came back to vandalize the church building.

During Christmas time Halcyonites gather together to celebrate and to sing Christmas carols. They exchange Christmas gifts at the Hiawatha Lodge. Christmas trees are decorated in The Temple and the Hiawatha Lodge. Christmas is a special time to remind everyone of the sacred birth of Jesus Christ.

The Halcyon Gift Store and Halcyon Post Office are unique. The Halcyon Store is one hundred years old as of 2008. Many remarkable and unusual gifts are displayed in the store. This Halcyon Store is remarkable because of the special gifts and atmosphere inside and exterior. The present building was built in the 1930s. The roof and walls have been restored and repainted with bright colors. The Halcyon Store is a landmark in San Luis Obispo County.

Halcyon is one of the most natural and beautiful places in California. Each home is unique. Gardens in Halcyon are beautifully cared for with flowers, trees and grass. Halcyonites take pride in upkeeping their dwelling places. Halcyon streets have been paved. There are no street lights or sidewalks. Halcyon should remain as it is with its natural environment and peaceful setting.

Twenty-Nine

Fruits and Vegetables

Fruits and vegetables are needed in order to provide fresh, raw food for people to eat. There are a wide variety of fruits and vegetables.

There are fruit and vegetable stands along roadsides where people can purchase an assortment of fresh fruits and vegetables. Grocery stores and supermarkets provide fruits and vegetables in a special section in each store.

Fruits and vegetables need to be kept clean by spraying cold water on them to keep them fresh. Some fruits are oranges, grapefruits, strawberries, pineapples, peaches, pears, grapes, cantaloupes, honey melons, lemons, pomegranates, cherries, figs, blueberries, apples and cranberries and more.

Tropical fruits are mangoes, bananas, papayas, breadfruit, kiwi fruit and more. Tropical fruit is plentiful in the tropics. Many people enjoy eating fresh, cut fruit. Mixed fruit dishes are very tasty and nutritional. Milk shakes are made with bananas, pineapples, oranges, berries and grapes. Each fruit is used in a milk shake. The fruit is ground up and mixed with milk and sugar. A mild shake mixer shakes up the milk and fruit until it thickens enough. These milk shake drinks are very delicious providing nourishment and energy.

Many vegetables are available in food stands and grocery stores. There are string beans, squash, dark green lettuce, carrots, tomatoes, cucumbers, okra, cabbage, parsley, watercress, garlic, onions, corn, eggplant, Brussels sprouts, regular sprouts, radishes, green and red peppers and more.

Vegetables produce vitamins and nutrients. Many of them have enzymes and chlorophyll in them. Fruits produce vitamin C and citric acid. There are enzymes in many fruits. We should eat fruits and vegetables very day to maintain good health.

Thirty

Greyhound Bus Journeys

People who do not have cars, vans or trucks travel by Greyhound buses to long distances. Greyhound buses are available in cities and towns across America.

Tickets must be purchased at bus stations before passengers can board assigned Greyhound buses. Passengers can select the seat they will travel in unless the bus is crowded. Then passengers must sit in whatever available seats are available.

Greyhound bus schedules are planned. Buses depart at given times and arrive at specific destinations at certain times. Bus drivers do their best to keep their travel schedules so their buses would be on time.

Greyhound bus drivers stop briefly for 15 or 20 minute breaks. Passengers are allowed to leave their assigned bus to use public bathrooms and to get snacks and fast food meals to go or to eat in the bus.

The seats in Greyhound buses are generally comfortable. Seats recline so passengers can sit back more comfortably. Passengers are able to look out windows at scenic views. Window views are usually worth observing because scenic views are very interesting and beautiful. Changing scenery is fascinating to observe while passengers look out the bus windows.

Thurston Wendon who lived in San Diego, California decided to travel across America by Greyhound buses. He wanted to save on gasoline and oil in his car. He decided it would be best to avoid wear and tear on his car.

Thurston packed one suitcase with clothes, nightwear, shoes and miscellaneous items such as shaving equipment, combs, toothbrushes and toothpaste, etc. He took a public bus from his home to the San Diego Greyhound Bus Station. Thurston purchased tickets to pay for a journey across the state of California.

The Greyhound bus was scheduled to leave at 8:30 a.m. from San Diego to Los Angeles, California. Thurston boarded the bus at 8:20 a.m. after he checked his suitcase at the storage section below the bus. He entered the bus and walked to a seat near a window near the front of the bus in the right side of the bus.

The scenery from San Diego to Los Angeles was interesting. Many orange groves and pine forests were visible along the freeway. The fragrance of oranges and orange blossoms was refreshing. Thurston opened his window so he could smell the orange trees as well as pine trees.

Finally, the Greyhound bus arrived in Los Angeles. The passengers were given a half hour break. Thurston had lunch in the Greyhound station. There were fresh sandwiches, potato chips and cold drinks in food machines. He sat on a bench in the Greyhound stations and ate a tuna sandwich, potato chips and he drank a can of root beer, which he purchased from food machines. Thurston went to the public bathroom in the Greyhound station. He had to hurry so he wouldn't miss his bus. He ran to the bus because his time was up.

Passengers were boarding the Greyhound bus. Thurston returned to his seat near the window. He was relieved that he made it back to his bus before it left. His next destination was from Los Angeles to Santa Barbara, California.

Thurston observed many open fields once the Greyhound bus was moving outside the city of Los Angeles. Thurston noticed farms and fields of farm land where vegetables were growing in rows. Some fields were being watered with sprays of water. Water was splashing into rows.

The Greyhound bus passed more groves of oranges. Then grapevines appeared. Many green grapevines were visible. No grapes were growing on the vines yet. Thurston observed the changing scenery. He finally fell asleep in his chair for a while. The bus continued on it route to Santa Barbara. The bus finally arrived at Santa Barbara Greyhound Station which was much smaller than the Los Angeles bus station. Everyone had an hour for dinner. Thurston woke up when he felt the bus stop. He realized that he was in Santa Barbara.

Thurston left the Greyhound bus and walked out of the bus station to find a restaurant nearby. He came to a Mexican restaurant. He went in and sat at a table near a window. He ordered cheese enchiladas, beans and rice and a salad with green lettuce, tomatoes and carrots with a salad dressing. He looked around the Mexican restaurant while he waited for his Mexican dinner. Mexican guitar music was being played. His dinner finally was brought to his table by a dark haired woman dressed in a waitress uniform. She appeared to be a Mexican lady. She smiled at Thurston.

Thurston decided to greet the waitress. He said, "Hello. Thanks for bringing my dinner." The waitress continued to smile. She replied, "I hope you enjoy your dinner." Thurston responded, "It looks delicious."

The waitress walked away and went into the kitchen at the Mexican restaurant. Thurston hoped she would visit more with him. He was disappointed because he wanted someone to visit with. He didn't socialize on the bus from San Diego to Santa Barbara. Thurston began eating his Mexican dinner of cheese enchiladas, beans, rice and salad. He enjoyed the Mexican food.

After dinner Thurston decided to walk around. He walked to the main street in Santa Barbara. He looked around at downtown shops. He went into several exotic shoe shops and enjoyed looking at artistic displays, artifacts and clothes. He found a colorful neck scarf made of wool. He purchased this neck scarf. He wore the scarf around his neck.

Thurston decided to stay in Santa Barbara for several days and nights. He arranged to take another Greyhound bus in several days. Thurston went to a downtown hotel close to the Greyhound station to stay for two nights. The next morning Thurston went to the Mission of Santa Barbara. He went into the chapel where he observed paintings of the fourteen Stations of the Cross. He saw statues of Jesus, Mother Mary and some of the saints and apostles. Thurston was impressed with the interior of the Mission chapel. He walked through the church museum next and witnessed many Spanish church artifacts and Indian collections.

Thurston took a city bus to the beach. He strolled on the white sand near the ocean. He enjoyed the ocean breeze. There were people walking on the beach. Some children and adults were playing volleyball. Other beach roamers were walking their dogs. Some of them threw Frisbees back and forth on the beach.

Thurston walked into shallow, ocean water to comfort his feet. He felt the rhythm of the ocean currents caress his feet. Thurston continued to stroll in the ocean water until he came to the Santa Barbara Pier. Thurston stepped out of the water and walked to the pier entrance. He put his shoes back on and began walking on the pier.

The Santa Barbara Pier was built with wooden planks and thick wooden poles. Big nails were nailed into the closely placed, thick planks. Thurston walked on the pier towards the deeper part of the ocean. He saw seagulls hovering over the pier. Some seagulls landed on pier poles and fence ledges on the pier.

There were boats in the harbor spread out in the ocean. Thurston walked up to a seafood restaurant on the pier. He walked into the restaurant and was taken to a table near a large window. The ocean view was spectacular. More seabirds were flying around over the ocean. Thurston enjoyed the spectacular view of the Santa Barbara Bay. He ordered a seafood lunch with French fries and cole slaw. He sipped a diet Pepsi.

After lunch Thurston walked back to the beach. He walked on the beach for a while. He got on a city bus and went to the Santa Barbara Zoo. He saw gorillas, monkeys, zebras, a lion, a tiger, some flamingoes, a few snakes and turtles, etc. The animals appeared well fed and safe. However, their cages were small except for the monkeys' cage. It was much larger so the monkeys could climb around. Thurston felt sorry for the caged animals in small cages.

Thurston went back to his hotel in downtown Santa Barbara. He went to his hotel room to rest and watch television for several hours. He walked downtown and selected an Italian restaurant to eat dinner. Thurston ordered a gourmet pizza, some spaghetti and a green salad. He sipped a root beer. The Italian restaurant was cozy and warm. Italian music was playing. Other people were eating pizza and spaghetti.

The next morning Thurston decided to continue his Greyhound trip up the West Coast. He sat by a window and observed the Pacific Ocean and surrounding harbors and beaches along the California coast. The Greyhound bus stopped in Santa Maria, California briefly for 20 minutes. Thurston only had time to use a public bathroom. He picked up a quick burger before he returned to the Greyhound bus.

The bus driver urged everyone to get back on the bus. He drove the bus along Highway One after he left Morro Bay. The coast was even more spectacular. Morro Bay Rock stood out to the passengers. San Simeon Bay was scenic. Hearst Castle could be seen high up on a hill above the ocean.

Thurston was enchanted with Carmel and Monterey which were along the California Coast. Pine trees added to the beautiful settings. Charming cottages exist in Carmel. Cottages were spread apart. The expansive, pristine beaches could be seen as a panoramic view near the ocean in Carmel.

Monterey was intriguing with its many seaside shops and seafood restaurants. Thurston met a lady on the Greyhound bus who was in her mid twenties. She was attractive and she had reddish-blonde hair and blue eyes. She was approximately 5 feet 5 inches tall. She had a slender figure.

Thurston introduced himself to the young lady. She sat near him in the bus from Morro Bay on. Thurston was 32 years old with brown hair and brown eyes. He was 5 feet 9 inches tall. He had strong, muscular arms. He was slender and he was wearing a casual, sports jacket, shirt, slacks and leather shoes. The young lady was wearing a lavender dress, white shoes and a cardigan, gold, button down sweater over her dress.

Thurston was attracted to Sally Williams. He observed how vivacious and gracious she was. Her blue eyes sparkled with warmth and light. Thurston spoke to Sally first. He said, "I'm from San Diego. I am traveling along the California Coast to see the sights. Where are you going?" Sally replied, "I am going to San Francisco." Thurston responded, "I am going to San Francisco. There are many adventures to experience in San Francisco."

Thurston and Sally continued to become acquainted on the bus. Scenic views were available along the way. Thurston invited Sally to have lunch with him in Monterey. They walked to the famous seafood restaurant at Fisherman's Wharf in Monterey called Rappas.

The Rappas Restaurant was at the end of the pier. Seals could be seen sunning themselves on a barge. Boats were floating in the harbor. Seagulls and pelicans were flying around the harbor and near the pier. Thurston and Sally sat near the windows where they could enjoy a marvelous view of the Monterey Harbor.

Thurston became even more well acquainted with Sally. She told him she lived in Morro Bay. She was a nurse at a hospital in San Luis Obispo. Thurston told Sally he was a Science teacher at a high school in San Diego. Thurston found out that Sally was a vocal soloist at a church in Morro Bay. She could play tennis, volleyball and golf. She played the piano and she played classical pieces with mastery.

Thurston and Sally continued to San Francisco on a Greyhound bus. They continued up the California Coast and they enjoyed scenic views of the harbors along the coast. The deep, blue sea was appealing to view. Waves rolled and crashed to shore on many beaches.

Once Thurston and Sally arrived in San Francisco they toured around the city to enjoy art galleries, museums, restaurants and historical sites. They saw Quoit Tower, Lombard, the twisting, spiral street, Fisherman's Wharf, the Golden Gate Park and they went to films at theaters. San Francisco was an enchanting city.

It was finally time to return south to Thurston and Sally's homes. Sally planned to go back to Morro Bay. Thurston planned to return to San Diego. They had spent a week together. Thurston had become fond of Sally. He wondered how they would continue to date each other once they returned to their homes.

Thurston told Sally he wanted to continue dating her. Sally responded with warmth and appreciation. Thurston said goodbye to Sally at the Morro Bay Greyhound Station. He told her he would call her soon. He planned to come visit her in the near future. Then Thurston kissed Sally affectionately and said, "I love you Sally." Sally smiled and said, "I love you, too."

Thurston kept in touch with Sally. He came to Morro Bay to be with her. They fell deeply in love. Thurston asked Sally to marry him after knowing her six months. Sally accepted Thurston's proposal of marriage. They were married in Morro Bay in June. Sally came to San Diego to live with Thurston after they were married. They had met on a Greyhound bus journey. Now they would be together for the rest of their lives.

THIRTY-ONE

FACING OBSTACLES

Everyone must face obstacles in their lives. Unexpected tragedies, dangers, illness and hardships may occur at any time. Life on Earth is temporary and it may be challenging because of obstacles.

A person may acquire handicaps and illnesses. Handicaps such as blindness, paralysis of muscles causing a person to become crippled and difficulty of hearing and speech can be obstacles to face. Poverty caused from unemployment can cause starvation and homelessness. Many people are homeless because they cannot afford to buy a home or to pay high rents. They live in alleyways, fields and shelters. Cold, dangerous streets in cities are not safe to dwell in at night.

Sharon Delgato was homeless, middle-aged woman who dwelled in New York City. She had a shopping cart which she kept her belongings in. She wore ragged clothes and a scarf on her head. She had dirt on her skin because she hadn't taken a shower or bath for many months.

Sharon was unemployed and she had to find food every day in order to keep from starving. She looked for scraps of food at restaurants and even in garbage cans. She received some food at a church which provided a cooked meal three days a week. Sharon stayed alive from the nourishment she received during these three meals each week. She didn't eat on alternate days when meals were not available.

Nights in New York City are very cold in autumn and winter months. Sharon had to endure the severe, cold weather. It snowed on the streets. Sharon had to find shelter under the eaves and alleyways. She covered herself with blankets. She wore an old coat with a raincoat over the coat. Sharon was cold at night. She sat in the alleyway waiting for the sun to come up. She often shivered from the coldness.

As time went on Sharon continued to survive in the streets of New York City. She wasn't strong enough to find a job. When she tried to get a job she was unable to keep it.

Sharon finally went to a shelter in New York City. She was given a cot to sleep on in a big room. Other homeless people stayed in the shelter. Sharon tried to get along with them. Some of the homeless people were friendly. Some of them were not friendly. Sharon didn't worry about being robbed. She didn't have any money. Her clothes were old and ragged.

Sharon had to face challenges every day. She needed to keep safe and find enough food to live. She needed to keep warm enough so she could stay alive. She couldn't afford to go to a doctor if she became ill. She had to cope with other homeless people who were ill with colds, flu, bronchitis or other diseases. Sharon lived to the age of 58. One day Sharon came down with pneumonia. She didn't go to see a doctor. Her pneumonia got worse and worse. Sharon suddenly passed away one night because of congestion in her lungs. She had struggled to survive. If she had been hospitalized in time she may have lived longer.

Henry Jolman faced obstacles in his life. He was borne with no arms. As a result it was difficult for him to be independent. His parents took care of him day and night. He had to be fed and dressed. He was unable to write. When he went to school he learned to read. He could read orally in class. He was unable to do seatwork.

Without a college education Henry was limited in what he could do for a living. Without hands he was handicapped. He faced the obstacle of needing personal care every 24 hours. Truthfully he was unable to get a job even in manual labor. Without hands he was not able to do much of anything.

Henry was finally put on disability Social Security when he was an adult at age 21. He was able to talk and communicate well enough to be understood. He could relay messages verbally. He watched television and listened to the radio. He could tell jokes and stories to his classmates and acquaintances.

Henry lived with his parents until he was 45. When both of his parents passed away he had to be placed in a home for disabled adults. He was surrounded by other disabled men and women. He knew he would never be able to get married or hold a regular job. He realized that he would have to cope with being disabled his whole life.

Thirty-Two

Train Experiences

Amtrak trains are generally a form of public transportation today. Tickets are purchased at the Amtrak station before passengers board the train.

There are two stories with passenger seats and window views on every Amtrak train. The seats are adjustable with recliners built in each seat. Most passengers want to sit near the windows to see the scenery along the way to their destination.

Passengers are allowed one piece of luggage with them. Other luggage is stored in the luggage section. There are three seats adjoined in each row on both sides of the train, the top floor is where passengers can purchase fast food. Trains are larger than public buses. Passengers can move around and they have more walking space. The windows are much larger. So, passengers can see views better.

It is generally cheaper to travel by train than by car. There are tables downstairs and upstairs. Passengers eat at the tables. They can play cards. They read newspapers and magazines. A train provides efficient, smooth motion. A train travels around 60 miles an hour on a track.

As long as the tracks are properly built and checked for safety a train is usually safe on the tracks.

Trains were created in the 1800s originally. There are cargo and passenger trains. Trains are still needed. Many people still depend on traveling by trains. They are able to go long distances on trains. Trains are kept away from freeways. Some trains travel near the oceans and over mountainsides.

Trains are valuable in the world. They should be preserved and people can travel by train to experience a relaxing and worthwhile experience.

Thirty-Three

Hollow Trees

Hollow trees have openings in their trunks. Redwood trees at Big Sur in California have hollow openings in very thick trunks. The hollow sections are caused by fires. Trees are partly burned by forest fires.

Several very tall, wide, redwood trees at Big Sur are so large that cars can drive through them. Hollow trees exist in forests around the world. Bigfoot creatures have hidden in hollow trees in forests in remote places.

Trees provide shelter and protection for animals and human beings. During rainstorms trees help keep rain off of animals and people. Hollow trunks can become shelters for people who are seeking shelter and possible safety.

Primitive people dwelled in hollow trees in different forests in ancient times. Trees provided shade from sunshine. American Indians ate acorns from certain trees. Tree leaves were used for food. Tree branches could be climbed to sit in. Primitive people climbed into trees with big branches to escape from wild animals. They slept in trees on branches during the night time especially when it became dark outside.

Hollow trees could be used for homes or dwelling places. Earlier peoples lived in forests. They took shelter in tree hollows as tribes. Mothers nursed their infants inside tree hollows. They kept their infants dry and warm inside tree hollows.

During cold autumn and winter months primitive tribes placed dry bark over hollow openings in trees. Bark shielded hollow openings in trees. Families could dwell in large, hollow openings. Fur bedding was placed on the floor of the hollow trees. Furs and animal skins kept people warm during windy days and nights. Bark coverings kept rain from blowing into the hollow tree shelters.

Campfires were used outside near the hollow trees so food could be cooked. Animals were captured and used for meat. Every animal skin was saved, cleaned, cured and made into clothes, twine, ropes, blankets and other items.

Hollow trees are valuable even today. Tourists travel to Big Sur to see hollowed out redwood trees. They drive their cars through some famous, hollowed out trees.

THIRTY-FOUR

ABUSES AND MISTREATMENT

Abusive behavior is common among gangs, lower class neighborhoods and homeless people. Children who are abused because their parents are violent and vulgar, tend to grow up with imbalanced and violent behavior to defend themselves.

Gangs may form with violent individuals. These groups of people join gangs in order to seek group power. Gangs tend to cause destruction especially in cities. Gang leaders control the gang usually.

Abuses cause individuals to behave irrationally. Violent actions cause injuries to occur. When a child is whipped and beaten up this causes shock and fear within him. A child learns to become violent because of abuse.

Hatred, anger, anxiety, doubts, fears and strong, negative reactions usually take place. Many children and adults are abused in the world. Children need to be understood and given guidance. They need to be treated properly with love, wisdom and respect.

Mistreatment during childhood can cause a child to become maladjusted. False beliefs and valued add to negative responses.

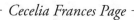

Generally, children who are treated with love, wisdom and respect grow up to be better, more adjusted adults. They learn to behave with self-control and balance. Well behaved individuals learn to treat other people with respect and decency.

THIRTY-FIVE

MYSTERIES IN ISRAEL

A mystery school existed in Jerusalem in Israel during the time of Jesus Christ. Jesus Christ mingled among the Essenes, who were an esoteric, religious group.

The Essenes were disciplined and they were deeply religious. The Essenes lived in houses together. They worked in the fields in the early morning hours. In the afternoons they did domestic chores. In the evenings they prayed and chanted.

Jews established the Jewish church in Israel. The Jews received The Ten Commandments when Moses brought them to the early Jews. He came down from Mount Sinai with The Ten Commandments which he received at a burning bush. Today it is believed by some that Moses was contacted by celestial beings who came in a flying saucer. The blazing light flashed from the flying saucer which appeared as a burning bush of flames.

The Jewish Temple in Jerusalem was the Temple of King David. A sacred chamber exists with the Torah and sacred, golden altar in the center of the sacred chamber. No one is allowed in this sacred chamber except several high priests once or twice a year. The energy of God is supposed to exist on this sacred altar.

Israel had been called the promised land for God's chosen people known as the Jews. The Israelites have existed for thousands of years. Jews have moved around from place to place for many years. Finally, after forty years the Jews migrated to Israel which became the promised land of the Jews.

Moslems also live in Israel. The Jews and Moslems try to get along. However many Moslems feel bitter because their land was taken away from them in Israel. Moslems feel their land should be returned to them. There has been a lot of tension and even bloodshed caused because of this injustice. Until Jews are willing to return the land they took away there will be continued tension and bloodshed.

Israel has developed. There is farming land where fruit trees, vegetables and some wheat, barley and olives are grown. The Israelites have prospered because of farming, fishing and trading goods as merchants. The Israelites depend on the support of the United States politically and even financially.

The American government spends millions of dollars in Israel. Americans are experiencing a financial crisis in the stock market. Banks, business establishments such as AIG and Lehman Brothers have become bankrupt. Other business establishments such as Morgan's Banking have taken over these companies that have become broke. The money given to Israel is needed in America.

The U.S.A. has oil wells in Israel. The Israelites are one of the only allies in the Middle East. This is why the American president, congress, senators and representatives support the Israelites.

Mysteries in Israel are also hidden in the Dead Sea Scrolls which were found in clay jars in desert caves. The Dead Sea Scrolls are kept in a museum today. These scrolls are being interpreted presently. Some of the teachings of Jesus Christ are in the Dead Sea Scrolls. He has written about metaphysical mysteries. Humanity has the opportunity to find out what was written in the Dead Sea Scrolls. Mysteries can be unfolded and understood.

Thirty-Six

The Mediterranean Sea

The Mediterranean Sea is located near Spain, France, Italy, Sicily, Sardinia, Mallorca which are west, north and east of the Mediterranean Sea. Morocco and Algeria are south of the Mediterranean Sea. Greece and Turkey are north of the Mediterranean Sea. Libya, Egypt and Jordan are south of the Mediterranean Sea. Israel, Lebanon and Syria are east of the Mediterranean Sea. Crete is in the Mediterranean Sea.

The Mediterranean Sea is an important sea because it touches many countries in Europe and Middle Eastern countries. Travelers can go on cruises on the Mediterranean Sea to many countries. This centrally located sea is well known and many boats, cruise ships and yachts navigate on this sea.

There are seaports in Spain, France, Italy, Sicily, Sardinia, Mallorca, Greece, Morocco, Algeria, Egypt, Israel, Lebanon, Syria and Jordan at the Mediterranean Sea. This sea is warm and pleasant to swim in near Spain, France, Sardinia, Corsica, Libya, Egypt, Israel and Syria. There are many, spectacular views of the Mediterranean Sea near the seashore of each country and island that borders this sea.

The Mediterranean Sea is deep and changes vivid colors of blue, turquoise, purple and light blue. Tourists look forward to boating on the Mediterranean Sea. Many cruise boats provide a vacation on the Mediterranean Sea.

Sailing, surfing, snorkeling and swimming are popular activities at the Mediterranean Sea. Many people stroll on beautiful beaches near the Mediterranean Sea. The Mediterranean Sea is the most popular sea in the world because it is located in an area near vacationland countries where many tourists come to enjoy their vacations and holidays.

Tourists will continue to enjoy the Mediterranean Sea. This popular sea provides an opportunity for many vacation activities for tourists and residents.

Barcelona is a bustling seaport in Spain near the Mediterranean Sea. Barcelona is an enchanting seaport with many red tile roofs, Valencia is another seaport city in Spain. Cartagena is another seaport in Spain. Tangiers is a seaport city in Morocco. Marseilles is a seaport city in France that many tourists go to for a vacation.

Athens is a seaport city in Greece near the Mediterranean Sea. Athens is well known in Greece which is the cradle of the Western World. Ancient Greek ruins such as temples and old columns and Greek statues exist near the harbor. Napoli and Rome are well known cities near the Tyrrhenian Sea close to the Mediterranean Sea.

The seaport city of Alexandria in Egypt is a historical land site. Ancient ruins exist in the Mediterranean Sea near Alexandria. Tel Aviv is a well known seaport city in Israel. Imports and exports are sent by ships to seaport cities near the Mediterranean Sea.

Crete is a well known island in the Mediterranean Sea. Many tourists go by boats to Crete for vacations. The climate is warm enough so tourists can go swimming and sailing. Sardinia is another island in the Mediterranean Sea. Tourists go to this resort island to bathe in the warm sea and to roam on the beaches. They enjoy fish dinners and festive activities such as folk dancing, singing and sunbathing.

It is worth traveling by cruise ships to the Mediterranean Sea to take in many seaport cities, beaches and seaport events and festivities. The climate is warm during spring and summer months. Tourists can come home with fond memories of their adventures and the many places near the Mediterranean Sea.

THIRTY-SEVEN

MYSTERY CAVES

Mystery caves exist in various locations near the ocean cliffs and mountainsides. There are many caves at Pismo Beach, Shell Beach and at Avila Beach near the Pacific Ocean in California.

Pirate Cove is located on a high hill overlooking Avila Beach Harbor. A large opening exists in Pirate Cove in the rocks on this scenic hill. A private beach exists below the rocky cave which is a cave to dwell in. many people drive up a narrow dirt road to go to Pirate's Cove. It was named after pirates who came to Avila Bay long ago.

Caves exist in cliffs near ocean tidepools above rocky ledges and sea beds. Ocean waves splash into these caves during high tide. People walk across the rocky terrain near the ocean to go into the caves hidden in the cliffs.

Clarence and Cynthia Tyman, who were hikers and beach strollers, decided to explore the caves near Pismo Beach. They walked onto a rocky area near the ocean. The tied was out so Clarence and Cynthia could observe tidepools. Some waves moved back and forth into several tidepools. They saw orange starfish and barnacles clinging to the rocks.

Small sea fish were swimming around the tidepools. Some of the fish were brightly colored and some were spotted. Crabs were crawling on nearby rocks and in the tidepools. Suddenly, some eels came into the tidepools when waves splashed into the tidepools.

Clarence and Cynthia continued to climb over the rough rocks carefully. They were wearing tennis shoes so they could walk easier over rocks and ledges. As they explored the cliffs they eventually came to some caves. Some of the caves were deep and wide. Other caves were much smaller.

Cynthia was curious and she wanted to explore these larger caves. She began walking in a deeper cave. Clarence followed Cynthia into this cave. It was darker towards the back of the cave. Cynthia came to a smaller pool of water. Small fish were moving around in the ocean pool. They were baby fish. This protective pool of ocean water was a safe place to dwell in.

Cynthia and Clarence saw barnacles on cave rocks. Some starfish were clinging to cave walls. The cave seemed safe and cozy. Cynthia decided to sit down on a rock ledge in the cave. Clarence sat down near Cynthia. They talked about their experiences on the beach, at the tidepools on the rocky area and what they saw in the cave.

Time went by while the Tymans sat in the cave. Suddenly ocean waves began to splash into the cave. Ocean water continued to flood the cave. Cynthia and Clarence stood up quickly and they tried to get out of the flooded cave. When they came to the entrance more waves were splashing into the cave. They were sopping wet and worried about getting out o the cave to the seashore again. They struggled to push past the ocean waves onto the rocky area where tidepools existed. The ocean water kept rising higher and higher.

Clarence and Cynthia had to start swimming in order to keep afloat in the ocean. They kept swimming swiftly against the ocean currents until they came to shore. Cynthia was worn out from swimming against the ocean currents. Clarence took her by her hands and assisted her out of the ocean. Cynthia decided to lay down on the beach to rest and to recover from her ordeal in the ocean.

Fortunately the sun was still shining. The sand was still warm. Cynthia was able to warm up on the beach. She was lying on the warm sand for some time to continue to recover. The sunlight warmed her body. Her clothes began to dry. Her long, black hair finally dried.

Clarence and Cynthia walked back to their car in Avila Beach parking lot. Clarence drove Cynthia home in Cayucos beyond Morro Bay to their home. They were glad to be safe in their home. They vividly recalled the dangerous experience they encountered in the hidden cave.

THIRTY-EIGHT

2012 A.D.

2012 A.D. is an important year in which ancient Mayans predicted the end of the Mayan calendar. All predictions for 5,000 years have taken place as predicted.

Some catastrophe or severe change may take place by December 21, 2012 A.D. according to the Mayans. Their round, stone calendar has specific, geometric carvings about each prediction step by step.

The Mayans predicted the exact date and time Hernando Cortez landed in Mexico. The Aztecs thought Cortez was the return of the white god Quetzlcoatl from the East. The Mayans predicted the eclipse of the moon in the 1990s at the Mayan temple of the Sun. On that day their Mayan gods from The Pleiades would return to the Mayan Temple of the Sun. They saw a silver, flying saucer with a dome on top over the Mayan temple.

The Mayans predicted the volcanic eruption of a big volcano right outside of Mexico City which took place in the 1990s. The Mayans predicted the end of the Mayan empire.

The Mayans predicted planetary alignments, floods and some

earthquakes. They prepared for the end of the Mayan civilization. They left their temples and villages and disappeared. Mayans no longer exist at the Mayan temples and villages in the jungles of Mexico.

The Mayans from Yucatan stretched to Belize in Central America in Honduras where their temples and Mayan cities once existed. They were mysteriously abandoned. The Mayans never returned again.

Mayans saw a star pattern where the Milky Way crosses the heavens as the "Crocodile Tree." The Mayans have told us that they have managed to find a way to get you to see that the future creates the present. They created the Mayan calendar with an end date. We are progressing toward this "End Time."

The Mayan calendar happens exactly where the dark cloud in the Milky Way begins a dark cloud of interstellar dust, the black hole of the Galactic Center. What is left of Earth's biological intelligence can pass into the Galaxy by going through this womb of darkness. "Now is the time to understand exactly how the Photon Band is the activation mechanism for the climax of the Mayan Great Calendar."

Seventeen sacred calendars of the Maya are described, most of which are short term cycles. One of the seventeen calendars shows a fifty Pleiadian cycle with the Sun orbiting around Alcyone in a 26,000 year, long cycle.

My vehicle noticed that the length of both the Pleiadian cycle and the precession cycle was 26,000 years and the end of the Mayan calendar and the precession into Aquarius were close in time.

Earth processes into Aquarius every 26,000 years when each Mayan Great Cycle completes and then begins again. According to both Aztec and Mayan cosmologies, 2012 is also the completion of a 104,000 year cycle composed of four Mayan Great Cycles. This coincides with the cycle of the Four Great Ages of the One who says Earth will be entering into the Fifth World. This cycle is also the completion of a 225 million year galactic orbit since the introduction of the reptile species on Earth.

As the Pleiadians have said, "At the end of the Great Calendar in 2012, biological intelligence will spread through the whole Galaxy by means of this information highway of light. It is as if these photon bands are stimulating antiparticles out of hiding in the whole Galaxy and then the photon force in the bands is increasing."

Mayans created the Mayan Great Calendar called the Tzolk'in to show you how to create a future intention, so you could decide what you want and work for these desires in the present time. The Mayans gave this calendar to our star system 104,000 years ago and our ancient journey with this calendar made us who we are today.

Many very respectable intellectuals are fascinated by the implications of the Mayan Calendar. It is a brilliant device that describes a process of time that approaches a completion point, the end of time. But this has nothing to do with the end of the world.

The Mayan Calendar is the ideal device to get men to become intuitive. The time has come for humanity to activate Gaia according to the Mayan Calendar.

According to the Mayan Calendar during the First Great Cycle 23,614 to 18,489 B.C. humanity began to observe themselves in their environment. In the Second Great Cycle 18,489 to 13,364 B.C. humanity went through a great and difficult leap in its evolution. During this phase humanity deposited many deep memories in their brains. Our solar system was far out in the Galactic Night during this Age of Scorpio from 17,280 to 15,120 B.C. when the great sky gods came to Earth.

The gods taught humanity how to follow the phases of the Moon with stone circles that indicated the time of eclipses and located where the Moon would rise and set. The shamans brought mushrooms into the stone circles and taught journeying with the spirits of the sacred plants. The spirits of these plants became humanity's teachers about the special places on the planet. Every valley, mountain and stream was sacred.

Before the gods left in 14,200 B.C. they showed humanity how to listen to the sounds of the Galaxy by drumming and rattling in bogs and swamps with amphibians, insects, reptiles and birds.

During the Third Great Cycle from 12,364 to 8239 B.C. humanity began to change as they always did when their solar system was in the Photon Band. Humanity learned to make stoner temples to enhance their energy so they could work with guardian spirits. Human beings became the people of the canyon, lake, high plateau and great mountain.

The age of Virgo was 12,960 to 10,800 B.C. We are now attaining what they knew in 11,000 B.C. before the Fall of Atlantis when humanity was given sovereignty over their own DNA. Many beings began to influence humanity.

The Fourth Great Cycle was 8239 to 3114 B.C. Earth women appreciated Anunnaki gods and goddesses for improving their minds. The Anunnaki came back in 3600 B.C. to institute patriarchy making a world based on themselves as male gods. They built great temples all over the Tigris and Euphrates valleys of Sumer. They brought Nibiruan cultural ideals to Earth which included language, writing and temple city cultures. From 3600 to 1600 B.C. the Sirians and NIbiruans brought technology working with humans to manifest ideas. They were both amazed by human creativity.

The Mayan culture brought to Earth was centered in the woman and home. The Mayan Calendar has the potential of attracting humanity to an illuminated world. The Mayans understood the Galactic Mind.

The present shift in consciousness in individuals and groups actually began with Baktun 12 of the Mayan Calendar from 1618 to 2012 A.D. This transformation continues to develop within humanity.

2012 A.D. may be the end of the Mayan Calendar. Yet humanity has the opportunity to continue to become illumined and awakened to truth and knowledge. A new cycle can take place for humanity with hope, faith and peace.

THIRTY-NINE

RESOLVING MISUNDERSTANDINGS

Misunderstandings often cause emotional stress and strong emotional reactions. Lack of communication adds to the misunderstandings. Hurt feelings brew up when critical, unkind, sarcastic remarks are said to sensitive people. Misunderstandings can lead to anger, frustration, scorn, hatred and argumentation.

Selena Cox was the eldest daughter in a family of eight children. She was busy helping her parents with household chores, cooking and gardening. Selena did her best to keep the family house neat and clean. She washed the family laundry and fed family pets. She even helped by taking care of her younger brothers and sisters.

One day while Selena was taking care of her little sisters, Alice who was two years old and Mary who was three were messing up the kitchen floor. Selena yelled at them and spoke harshly to them. She said, "Stop messing up the kitchen floor!" The two younger sisters continued to mess up the floor. Selena walked over to the toddlers. She snapped her fingers at them. The girls began to cry.

Selena's mother, Mrs. Cox, who was upstairs, heard Alice and Mary crying loudly. She rushed downstairs to find out why they were crying. As Mrs. Cox appeared in the kitchen she saw Selena spanking each of the girls.

Mrs. Cox came over to Selena. She said, "What is going on? Why are you spanking Alice and Mary?" Selena stopped spanking the girls. They continued to cry for a period of time. Mrs. Cox spoke to Selena. "Don't spank Alice and Mary!"

Selena looked at her mother with a hurt expression. She walked out of the kitchen and went to her bedroom. She sat down on her bed and thought about the way her mother spoke to her especially in front of Alice and Mary. She thought her mother undermined her authority in front of her little sisters. She felt her mother should have accepted her form of discipline. She felt misunderstood by her mother.

Selena stayed in her bedroom for several hours. She tried to recover from the episode with her mother. She listened to the radio and she tried to relax.

Mrs. Cox finally came upstairs to check on Selena. She walked into Selena's bedroom and looked at her. Mrs. Cox realized that her daughter was offended because she had criticized her. Selena's mother said, "Selena, are you alright?"

Selena looked at her mother with a frown on her face. She remained silent with a sullen expression. Selena's mother said, "Alice and Mary are taking a nap. I spoke to them about the mess they made on the kitchen floor. I believe they will not make such a mess again."

Selena still appeared sullen. Then she spoke. "You made me feel bad about spanking Alice and Mary! They would not obey me. So I spanked them!" Mrs. Cox replied, "Alice and Mary appeared very upset. This is why they cried so long! I realize you only wanted to discipline the girls. Try to reason with the girls before you spank them."

Selena stood up from her bed. She said, "If they disobey me again I intend to spank them again if they continue to disobey me!" Selena's mother responded, "Be careful how you spank them. They are only toddlers. They don't understand."

Selena said, "If I am expected to take care of Alice and Mary they must obey me! They need to be spanked so they will mind me!" Mrs. Cox realized that Selena felt she did what she had to do so Alice and Mary would obey her. She replied, "I appreciate that you are helping to take care of the girls. I hope they obey you."

Selena began to look better. Her mother was beginning to understand why she spanked her little sisters. She was glad her mother began to understand her approach to discipline. This issue was finally resolved.

FORTY

T.V. Dinners and Frozen Foods

T.V. dinners and other frozen foods are popular. There is a wide selection of T.V. dinners and other frozen foods. The food is placed in aluminum packages and special cardboard paper wrapping with pictures and labels describing the food.

Shoppers can select cheese enchiladas, beans and rice, tamales, beans and rice, spaghetti and meatballs, chicken, mashed potatoes, string beans and steak, macaroni, mixed vegetables and many more selections. Chinese food can be put into T.V. dinners. Beef Stroganoff with cut carrots and celery cooked in it, pot roast with a variety of cooked vegetables such as potatoes, carrots, celery, string beans and corn kernels are more prepared foods.

Other frozen foods are containers of corn, string beans, peas, carrots, mixed vegetables, cheese and macaroni, Spanish rice, hash brown potatoes and potatoes au gratin. These foods are easy to prepare once they are unwrapped. Vegetables are prepared in boiling water. Macaroni and cheese and potatoes au gratin can be heated up in the oven. Spanish rice is warmed up in a pan with some water. Hash brown potatoes are sautéed in a frying pan before they are served.

Frozen foods and T.V. dinners are easily prepared without much effort. No personal cooking is required. Food can be put in a microwave oven within minutes and served for lunch or dinner.

Today housewives can use frozen foods and T.V. meals readily for lunch and dinner if they don't have time to prepare meals from scratch. They can buy pies, cakes, pudding and Jello for dessert. A whole meal can be heated up and served within a short time.

We live in an era with many, modern conveniences. Food is prepared quickly without careful preparation because of frozen foods and T.V. dinners. Frozen foods and T.V. dinners can be preserved in freezers and heated up in the oven and in pans whenever needed.

FORTY-ONE

AUSTRALIAN FASCINATIONS

Australia is the largest, island continent in the southern hemisphere. There are eight provinces which are Queensland, New South Wales, Victoria, South Australia, West Australia, Northern Territory and Australian Capital Territory. The island of Tasmania is another province.

The capital of Queensland is Brisbane. The capital of New South Wales is Sydney. The capital of Victoria is Melbourne. The capital of South Australia is Adelaide. The capital of West Australia is Perth. The capital of Northern Territory is Darwin. The capital of Australian Capital Territory is Canberra. The capital of Tasmania is Hobart.

Australia is surrounded by the South Pacific Ocean. New Zealand is a smaller island near Australia. Australia was connected to other, large continents at one time.

The Gold Coast is well known as a surfer's paradise near Brisbane. Many surfers go to the Gold Coast to perform on different surfboards. Some surfers surf on very high waves. The ocean warms up in the summer. Boating is common at the Gold Coast. There are yacht races frequently. Tourists and beachcombers can observe sailing boats in races while they gaze out to sea from long, pristine beaches.

Ayers Rock is the largest rock known in the world. It is located in Central Australia in a hot desert. Aborigines live near Ayers Rock. Dingoes dwell near Ayers Rock. Ayers Rock is a landmark in the world. It is made of red, lava rocks.

Tourists travel to Ayers Rock and some people climb up its slopes on a specific trail. It takes a group of hikers hours to reach the top of Ayers Rock. They dress in lightweight, cool clothing because the blazing sun is very hot. The view from the tip is spectacular. Tourists can see for miles across the desert.

Tourists camp out near Ayers Rock. Dingoes run around the desert in packs hunting for food. They hunt for rodents, birds' eggs and snakes. Dingoes sneak into tourists' camps to steal food. Tourists must be on guard. They have to keep their food packed in their car trunks especially at night. They must keep a close watch on their young children.

Blue Mountains are very picturesque inland from Sydney in New South Wales. Trees with blue leaves exist in forests in this region. The atmosphere is very clear and fragrant with pine trees and wild flowers.

James Cook, a sea captain from England, landed at Botany Bay on April 29, 1770 in Australia. The first penal colony developed at Port Jackson in January, 1788 under the command of Captain Arthur Phillip who became the colonists' first governor. The colonists moved to Parramatta to establish crop farming.

The colony expanded west by traveling over the Blue Mountains in 1813. An inland route was developed to New England in 1823 and in 1827 to the Darling Downs. When English colonists were liberated they continued to explore Australia.

Sydney, the state capital of New South Wales, is a vibrant, cosmopolitan city today with one of the most magnificent harbors in

Australia. Sydney has many attractions such as luxury hotels, a wide choice of restaurants, historical sites and lively nightlife.

From a touring point of view the rest of the state of New South Wales is divided into nine main, scenic areas. They are known as the North Coast, the Hunter Region, and the New England Region to the north of Sydney, the Western Slopes and Western Plains to the west and the South Coast, Southern Highlands, Riverina and Snowy Mountains to the south.

If you continue north past the Central Coast you will come to two spectacular waterways, Lake Macquarie and Port Stephens. Newcastle, the second largest city in New South Wales is near these lakes. These beautiful, picturesque lakes are deep blue.

Another vivid attraction is the vineyards in Hunter Valley near Pokolbin, Australia's oldest wine growing region. Other attractions include the magnificent mountains and woodlands of Barrington Tops as well as the interesting, historic towns of Maitland and Stroud.

If you travel along the coast to Queensland, the North Coast of New South Wales unfolds as a vacationer's paradise. This region presents a combination of subtropical climate, lush river valleys and sunny, golden beaches. Port Macquarie, Kempsey, Coffee Harbor, Byron Bay and Grafton are unique and appealing especially for tourists and vacationers to enjoy.

The England Plateau is Australia's highlands region where the landscape ranges from spectacular mountain scenery from the Great Divide Range to rich wheatlands in the west. The center of this region is the beautiful university town of Armidale. Tamworth, also in the highlands, is Australia's Nashville, the country and western music capital.

The country is more sparsely populated in rural areas past the Blue Mountains. The first town settled west of the range is Bathurst, known as a relaxed country town. It is surrounded by attractive, rolling countryside and sheep properties.

You can visit the ghost gold mining town of Hill End, known for gems. You can taste wines in Mudgee's Vineyards and inspect the largest radio-telescope in the Southern Hemisphere at Parkes. Western Plains, Dubbo has a unique zoo where exotic animals roam free. In Lightning Ridge you can look for opals.

The state floral emblem, the Waratah (telopea Speciosimma) is a beautiful red flower which blooms in New South Wales. The state's Outback region, which occupies two-thirds of New South Wales has unique landscape.

Like an oasis in a desert, the mining town of Broken Hill, home of the Flying Doctor Service, is a garden city surrounded by four national parks. Spectacular bird exist in this region.

South of Sydney are panoramic headlands and rolling beige-green hills around Kiama. The south is a succession of pretty, white beaches and secluded bays that overlook the shores of Jervis Bay, Sussex Inlet and St. George Basin. The whole coast is an angers' paradise. You can observe the busy, fishing port of Uleadulla. There are fabulous holiday resorts such as Batemans Bay and Merimbula which are surrounded by hidden coves. From Bermagui down to the colorful, old whaling port of Eden, this coast is renowned for game fishing.

The Southern Highlands is a lush pastoral area with magnificent national parks. Berrima, one of Australia's best preserved colonial towns is an interesting, historical town. Scenic highlights of the region include Fitzroy, Belmore and Carington Falls and Kangaroo Valley, a luxuriant farming area which you can also reach from Berry on the coast.

Mt. Kosciuszko is Australia's highest mountain. Snow skiing is popular at this mountain. The main ski resorts are Thredo, Perisher and Smiggin Holes. Thredo has the steepest slopes and a captivating, alpine atmosphere. This area is also beautiful in summer with excellent trout fishing at Lake Jindabyne and Eucumbene. There are very scenic drives around Tumut and Khancoban.

To the west of the Snowy Mountains lies the fertile agricultural region named the Riverina after two great rivers, the Murrumbidgee and the Murray. The center of the Murrumbidgee Irrigation Area is Griffith surrounded by a patchwork of rice fields, vineyards and orchards. Tourist activities in the Riverina revolve around visiting food processing plants and wineries. Leeton offers hot air ballooning and from Moama you can cruise along the Murray.

New South Wales has sixty-eight national parks which offer an astounding variety of topography and vegetation from rainforests and coastal wilderness to sand dunes, flat red plains, mangrove swamps and alpine woodlands. Bush walking, camping and whitewater rafting are some of the activities available in the parks.

Sydney is a magnificent harbor city with the Sydney Tower, the tallest structure in the Southern Hemisphere. The Sydney Harbor Bridge is a well known bridge in Sydney. You can stroll along Macquarie Street towards the Opera House, Sydney's most elegant and historical avenue. Macquarie Street is lined with beautifully restored colonial buildings.

Hyde Park Barracks houses exhibitions of early Sydney. The Parliament House is cinnamon and rose painted. The Grecian-style edifice on the corner is the State Library of New South Wales which contains the world's best collection of Australia.

A stroll along Macquarie Street brings you to the Royal Botanic Gardens which sweep down to the harbor. The Tarpeian Way gives a superb view of the Opera House. On the other side of the Botanic Gardens stretches the domain, where orators shout from soap boxes on Sunday afternoons. In January during the Festival of Sydney, the domain throngs with music lovers who picnic while listening to free, open-air concerts.

At the eastern end Circular Quay on Bennelong Point stands the

Opera House with its eggshell shaped architecture. At the western end of Circular Quay, beneath Observatory Hill, lies a quaint warren of steep, twisting streets and cobbled lanes called The Rock. This was the site of Sydney's first barracks, hospital and prison and many of its early buildings and pubs have been attractively restored, including the 1840 Garrison Church and Cadman's Cottage, Sydney's oldest building. The Argyle Centre has become an interesting crafter center.

The newly restored Queen Victoria Building is a magnificent, art deco complex with exquisite galleries of interesting boutiques. The strand Arcade has Edwardian charm. The city's main shopping area is between King and Park Streets. It has been said that Sydney has more shops per head population than any city in the world.

The Powerhouse Museum is an exciting, modern museum. Around the corner near Dixon Street is Sydney's Chinatown which is a bustling area of oriental emporiums stocked with silks, spices and delicacies and restaurants serving every Chinese cuisine.

New South Head Road is a pleasant, tree-lined drive that sweeps around towards Watsons Bay past picturesque Rushcutters Bay, Double Bay and Rose Bay. Double Bay has classy boutiques, exotic cafes and a lively, cosmopolitan atmosphere.

Australia is a fascinating place to visit with its rugged terrain, subtropical locations, bays, waterfalls, deserts, snowy mountains and rainforests and resorts. So visit Australia.

Forty-Two

Life in Germany

Germany is a European country which is northeast from France. Switzerland, Austria, Czechoslovakia, Poland and Belgium border Germany. The North Sea is near Germany.

Two world wars have reduced Germany from a great European empire to a western European country smaller in size than France. As a result of World War II, Germany lost territory to Poland, France and Denmark, and surrendered all her possessions in Africa and the Pacific.

Although no treaty has yet been signed with the four Allied Powers, the defacto territorial transfers to the Soviet Union and Poland at Potsdam (1945) appear to be basically established. In 1949 separate governments were established for West and East Germany by independent action of the Allied nations and the Soviet Union respectively.

Today Germany has made political and social progress. Germany has become a democratic country. Major cities in Germany are Hamburg, Berlin, Frankfurt, Heidelberg, Munich and Leipzig. East Berlin has been freed from Communism. The Berlin Wall has been torn down.

The people of East Berlin are able to go to West Berlin and other places. For many years East Berlin was controlled by Communism. Today the liberation of the German people is taking place.

Heidelberg is a university city near the Black Forest. Many students come to the restored university. Heidelberg is a cultural center for Arts and Drama. This city is surrounded by many, evergreen trees.

Berlin is the capital city of Germany. Ronald Reagan brought down the Berlin Wall in 1989 to 1990 in Berlin. There are cultural centers where art museums, an opera house and cultural events take place.

Hamburg is a large city near the North Sea. Technology and Science are developing rapidly. There is an autobahn which are the most modern freeways in the whole world. There are no speed limits. Drivers can drive very quickly on the autobahn.

Frankfurt, which is in the central western part of Germany, is another emerging city of cultural opportunities. There are artists, poets and scholars in Frankfurt. The University of Frankfurt is one of the best universities in Germany. Many scholars who write research have graduated from this highly rated university.

Frankfurt is known for its factories and German wieners and schnitzel. The frankfurter is well known because it was created in Frankfurt. German cooking is unique. Many meat and potato recipes are used. Cabbage and corned beef, beef Stroganoff, German chocolate cake and German pastries add to German meals.

Germany is a clean country with many evergreen plants and trees. The Rhine River flows through Germany. It is the largest river in Germany. There are scenic castles on either side of the Rhine River. Many tourists and vacationers cruise in boats on the Rhine River. A lot of fresh water flows in the Rhine River.

Germans fish in the Rhine River for a variety of fresh water fish. They enjoy fish dinners as well as sausage and sauerkraut dishes. German families eat potato salad, chopped vegetables, homemade German bread and puddings. Many Germans drink German beers. There are light and dark beers. They drink beer in large, beer cups called steins.

Germans enjoy German dances. They dress up in traditional costumes. They enjoy folk dances. Many Germans love classical music. They go to operas and stage plays for cultural pleasure. German people are very intelligent and many of them are well educated. They have learned several languages and educational standards are high in German schools.

Germany is an up and coming European country. Germans use the European Euro. Their economy is thriving. Gasoline is high prices as in other European countries.

Some German hotels are very expensive during tourist season in the summer. Restaurant food tends to be expensive. Tourists need to be ready to pay higher prices for vacations in Germany. Tourists should study about tourist events and places by picking up travel booklets and brochures about German restaurants, resorts, cultural events and cultural opportunities.

Changes that have occurred in politics, governmental leadership, in the German economy and lifestyles in Germany are making a difference to visitors and tourists as well as to the German people. People from other countries such as Viet Nam, Iraq and other countries have moved into Germany to live and seek employment. This has caused some problems in the job market in Germany.

Germans are forced to accept people from foreign countries living in Germany. Some Germans do not accept so many foreigners populating their country. Foreigners have different attitudes and beliefs. They have an effect on the Germans and Germany.

The German government provides funds for schools, public services, roads, hospitals and upkeep of natural resources, etc. The job market is limited in providing employment for people. German citizens are also in need of employment. Foreigners should not take away their jobs and employment opportunities. Germany is a member of the United Nations.

German leaders speak up about their concerns and problems. They have a voice in world affairs. Many Germans have traveled to America for vacations. Some Germans have come to America to live. Their attitudes have gradually changed since World War II. Many Germans realize that Hitler and his German Nazis were wrong about exterminating the Jews. They realize that World War II changed their lives forever.

FORTY-THREE

JAPAN TODAY

Japan is on an island near Asia. Japan is mountainous. Earthquakes occur more frequently here. The capital city is Tokyo. Tokyo is one of the largest cities in the world. Many manufactured goods are produced in factories in and around Tokyo. The atmosphere is polluted with smog and burning substances in the air.

Other cities in Japan are Kyoto, Osaka, Nagoya, Sapporo, Matsuyama and Okayama, etc. Tokyo is located on the main island and largest island in Japan. There are cultural opportunities such as Geisha houses, Kabuki theaters and multiple, shopping malls. Tokyo is very populated. Many tourists come to this well known city in Japan. There are skyscrapers. Yet, there are parks and a large zoo.

Japanese men wear conservative, black suits. Many Japanese businessmen work in offices in downtown Tokyo. City streets are filled with many Japanese businessmen going to work and coming home from work. Japanese women also work in shops, restaurants, business offices and some work in Geisha houses in the city of Tokyo. They wear regular, western clothing. Japanese women look very modern in their western clothing and hairstyles. Some dye their hair and they wear makeup.

The islands of Japan are Hokkaido, Honshu, Shikoku and Kyushu. There are many smaller islands to the south of the larger Japanese islands, such as the Izu Islands, Ogasawara Islands and Goto Islands, and many more. Japan is located in the Sea of Japan. It is close to Korea. The Pacific Ocean is east of Japan.

Japanese people are hardworking and very industrious. They produce Japanese cars, household products and many electronic devices and manufactured goods. They have been very successful in selling their merchandise to other countries such as America, Europe, Australia, Pacific Ocean Islands, Canada, Alaska and different islands around the world.

The World's Fair took place in 1970 at Osaka. Many pavilions were set up and used to display the cultural life, arts and crafts, foods and traditional costumes of major countries. The World's Fair is sponsored in different countries. It takes place every few years in a different country. Thousands of people have traveled to Japan to attend the World's Fair. Tourism increased considerably in 1970.

Pearl diving, fishing and snorkeling for mussels and coral are popular in Japan. Pearls are found in oysters. There are large and small pearls which are either white or black. Pearls are sold in Japan at various prices. Some pearls are very expensive. Artificial pearls are also produced which are inexpensive. They are commercialized and made into pearl necklaces and bracelets. They are sold in jewelry shops and department stores.

Raw sushi which is called sashimi is popular in Japan. Japanese people eat a lot of raw fish. Raw sushi is exported to other countries because there is a surplus of sushi in Japan. Japanese dishes of kelp wrapped around white rice are served as rice cakes. Octopus, squid, oysters and shellfish are cooked and served at Japanese restaurants.

Kabuki theaters are well known especially in larger cities in Japan such as Tokyo, Kyoto, Nara and Kobe. Only male performers act on the stage. They impersonate Japanese women. Male actors paint their faces with white makeup and wear black, Japanese wigs and feminine kimonos. They act out feminine roles on the stage.

Kabuki theaters have existed for hundreds of years. Japanese dramas are acted out about different Japanese tales and stories. Japanese actors are very dramatic on the stage. They impress many audiences with their performances.

Japanese children start elementary school at five years of age. They are well educated in Japanese schools. They learn to speak English as well as Japanese. They learn to read and write in Japanese as well as in English. Japanese children are taken on field trips to cultural sites in Japan.

Japan is a thriving country of many economical, political and social diversities. Many people live in Japan today. Japan has become more of a western country. A Diet government exists in Japan after World War II. A Japanese emperor is the ruler. He oversees what is happening in the Japanese government.

Japan is affected by the world economy. The yen is used in Japan. Mount Fiji is the highest mountain in Japan. The Shinto religion is the main religion in Japan. Shinto followers hike up to the top of Mount Fiji for a pilgrimage at least once in a lifetime. Shintoism is about bridging the light of the sun. They believe in sun gods who created the universe and the Earth. Shinto gods are supposed to protect everyone and they promote prosperity and well being. Heaven is beyond a Shinto gate.

Japanese farmers grow rice and Japanese vegetables. They grow green tea in layered sections. Farmers cultivate and water the fields of rice and tea. They wear straw hats. They grow a lot of rice and tea. They export rice and tea to other countries.

Japan has become a progressive country because of its growing economy. Japan is a member of the United Nations. Japan competes by producing many commercial products. The Japanese people have become western and are aware of world issues.

FORTY-FOUR

NEW ZEALAND ENCHANTMENT

New Zealand is a smaller group of two islands near Australia. Auckland and Wellington are the largest cities in New Zealand. Wellington is the capital city of New Zealand. New Zealand is in the Pacific Ocean.

The landscapes and climate are diversified in New Zealand. There are fertile, verdant valleys and meadows with rich green grass and wild flowers. Pasture lands exist where sheep and cattle graze. Many beaches and coastal cliffs exist along the New Zealand coastlines. Mount Cook is a snowcapped mountain on the first island. Hot rocks exist in different harbors. Hot water flows up through the open rocks.

The weather changes even during one day. It may be warm and sunny in the morning and colder with rain in the afternoon. Sometimes it becomes windy. The rain is beneficial because it causes grass and plants to grow abundantly.

Many evergreen trees grow in forests in many places. There are pine and eucalyptus trees growing to add to the enchantment of the New Zealand landscape.

Scenic views of the ocean are magnificent along the New Zealand coast. The ocean is a deep blue with shades of turquoise and purple. In some coastal areas trees silhouette the ocean as vacationers drive past many, unusual ocean views. Scenic views are serene moments of bliss.

New Zealand has a thriving economy. The Governor-General is Anand Satyanand. The Prime Minister is John Key. The government of New Zealand works to promote peace and prosperity. It stays out of war issues. It does not interfere with problems in the East. The money in New Zealand is used to help the people of New Zealand prosper. New Zealanders receive more government benefits. As a result New Zealand has one of the best economies in the world.

The Maoris are an ancient, indigenous people who lived in New Zealand for many years. They came to New Zealand over a thousand years ago. They had a unique, primitive culture. They carved into teak wood and put their designs on walls in well built buildings. Maori women perform with white, woven balls on long strings in a dramatic manner. Men stick out their tongues and create fierce expressions on their faces to scare away enemies. They wear well designed native costumes.

New Zealand is an enchanting place to visit. There are activities such as swimming, surfing, snorkeling, boating, horseback riding, skiing at Mount Cook and touring around the islands. Couples can go out to dinner at interesting restaurants and go dancing at nightclubs and at hotel resorts. New Zealand is an ideal place to go for an exciting vacation.

Forty-Five

Importance of Motherhood

Motherhood is the most important role in the world. Mothers should be aware of proper nutrition especially during pregnancy and during breast feeding. A mother should remain healthy so she can take care of her children.

Mothers spend more time raising their children. They should set an example of proper behavior. Mothers teach their children manners. Mothers teach their children how to walk and talk. Clean language should be taught. Vulgar, unclean language should be avoided.

Children should learn self responsibilities early. Learning to dress oneself and tie one's shoes should be accomplished. Chores such as making one's bed, cleaning up one's bedroom, dusting the house, vacuuming the carpets, washing dishes, weeding the garden and mowing the lawn are some chores to learn to do. Children learn by participating at home by doing housework and gardening.

A mother has a lot of influence on her children. How she disciplines her children makes a difference in how they may turn out. A mother should guide each of her children so they become responsible citizens in society.

Mothers can influence their children to join community clubs such as Girl Scouts, Boy Scouts, 4-H, athletic clubs, book clubs, gardening groups, hiking clubs, dancing and music activities. Children need to participate in the home and community while they are growing up.

Mothers can attend PTA which is Parent Teacher Association at the schools where their children attend. A mother can become a leader at PTA. Her suggestions and ideas may be helpful at school. PTA members make decisions about school programs and activities. They may plan a school carnival or bonanza program. Mothers can organize school parties and festivals.

Mothers can teach their daughters how to cook. Girls should grow up learning to cook many recipes. Girls should learn to prepare meat, potatoes, salads, vegetables, bread and a variety of desserts such as pies, cakes, cookies, pudding, Jello and mixed fruit dishes.

Girls grow up and get married. They should know how to cook before they get married. Girls can learn a lot from their mothers about cooking and household responsibilities.

Motherhood is the most important responsibility in the world because children who are born will inherit the world. When they become adults they will behave according to their childhood upbringing. Children acquire their parents' habits and values. Mothers change the world by the way they raise their children.

Forty-Six

Fascinating Seacoasts

Many seacoasts exist around the world. Every continent has many seacoasts. Islands have many coastlines.

California has a long coastline on the West Coast. From San Diego to Eureka there are many beaches. Beaches with ocean views exist in San Diego, Oceanside, Newport Beach, Los Angeles, Ventura, Carpinteria, Point Concepcion, Santa Barbara, Oceano, Pismo Beach, Avila Beach, Morro Bay, Cambria, Big Sur, Carmel, Pacific Grove, Monterey, Santa Cruz, San Francisco, Fort Bragg, Eureka, Arcata and Crescent City.

Each of these coastal cities has scenic harbor views. Boats are in these harbors. Some beaches have piers. Oregon has a West Coast. Scenic views exist near the Pacific Ocean. Brookings, Carpenterville, Gold Beach, Port Orford, Bandon, Coos Bay, Winchester Bay, Westlake, Florence, Yachls, Wataport, Seal Rack, Newport, Agate Beach, Depoe Bay, Taft, Neskowin, Bay City, Pacit City, Sandlake, Netarts, Rockaway, Brighton, Wheeler, Manazanita, Cannon Beach, Seaside, Geartha and Astoria are coastal cities, towns and bays. They have scenic beaches with panoramic harbors.

Many people like to go to beaches and harbors to sunbathe, to swim, to go fishing and boating. People have picnics on the beach. They like to stroll along beaches. There are fascinating places to go in coastal harbors.

Washington is near the Pacific Ocean. Coastal locations in Washington are Seaview, Long Beach, Ocean Park, Bay Center, Takeland, South Bend, Grayland, Westport, Cosmopolis, Hoquiam, Copalis Beach, Pacific Beach, Moclips, Taholan, Lapush, C. Alava, Portage Head and Neah Bay. Each of these coastal locations offers a beach view and scenic harbor. People go boating, fishing and surfing in many of these bays and harbors.

Fascinating seacoasts exist in many places on the West Coast and East Coast of America. Coastal views add to the beauty of America. Rugged cliffs exist along many harbors. Pristine beaches are magnificent along many bays. Sunsets are spectacular with brilliant crimson, purple and yellow hues of reflected light. The sun gradually goes down over the horizon. The sun looks like a burning lantern as it settles below the ocean and disappears.

Seacoasts are wonderful havens to go to so you can enjoy seagulls, pelicans and sandpipers hovering in flocks on different beaches and in the sky. Seashells can be seen on the warm sand. Clams exist in the sand and in the ocean. Sand dollars are lying on many beaches. So, go to the seacoasts to appreciate natural settings. Listen to the waves and feel the rhythm of the ocean. Appreciate the gleaming sun on the sparkling ocean. Feel the warmth of the sun. Listen to the seabirds. Smell the salty sea air.

FORTY-SEVEN

MAURINE'S CHALLENGE

Maurine Alvarez was approaching ninety-five. She was able to walk without a cane. She had white hair and she had clear blue eyes. She dressed in a blouse and pants that matched with a warm sweater. She wore tennis shoes and a straw hat.

Maurine liked to go walking almost every afternoon. She walked on a pathway into some nearby woods. She felt the sun on her face and back. Maurine was careful to walk over rocks and stones in the pathway. She was used to walking for three miles several days a week.

Maurine maintained strength in her legs and body because she walked regularly. On rainy days she exercised indoors. She believed in taking care of herself. Even at ninety-five she could still drive a car. She was still independent. She lived in her home by herself.

Challenges occurred in Maurine's life. She lost her husband at the age of seventy-five. He was seventy-seven when he passed away. Maurine had to learn to live by herself after he was gone. She managed to clean house, cook and take care of her front and back yards. She liked to grow flowers such as daisies, roses and dahlias.

Maurine spent time cultivating her garden. She planted a vegetable garden. She loved to watch flowers blooming in her yard. She stood near the flowers to smell their fragrance. She loved nature and she liked to explore around when she went walking.

Neighbors were aware of Maurine. They knew her for years. They often noticed that she walked by their homes regularly. They assumed that Maurine was capable of walking by herself. Maurine continued walking every day. She even walked on rainy days. She wore her raincoat and rain hat and she used her umbrella to shield herself from rain.

Fortunately Maurine lived in California in San Diego where the climate is generally moderate and pleasant. So, Maurine did not have to walk in snow or hail. She remained healthy and strong even at the age of ninety-five. She appeared twenty years younger than she actually was. Maurine had a leak in her roof. She took a ladder over to the leaky section of the roof. She decided to climb the ladder to survey the leak in her roof.

While Maurine was checking for the leak in the roof she accidentally slipped on one of the rungs of the ladder. She lost her balance and she fell off the ladder at least ten feet. Maurine tumbled to the hard ground. She broke her collarbone and her left leg. Maurine was in severe pain.

Maurine screamed loudly for help. She hoped her neighbors would hear her. She was lying on the ground for thirty-eight minutes. Finally one of her neighbors heard Maurine calling for help. The neighbor came over into her side yard and saw Maurine helpless, lying on the ground.

The neighbor was Paul, a middle-aged man with gray hair, wearing a casual shirt and slacks. He said, "What happened to you, Maurine?" Maurine spoke. "I fell off my ladder. I can't get up. I think I broke my leg and neck." Paul said, "I will call an ambulance." He used his cell phone which he had with him. Paul called for an ambulance.

It took approximately twenty minutes for an ambulance to arrive.

Meanwhile, Paul brought over some blankets from his house to cover Maurine up to keep her warm. Maurine was in shock because of the pain in her neck and leg. She had never broken any bones in her body before.

Finally, the ambulance arrived. Paramedics brought a stretcher over to Maurine. They carefully lifted her into the stretcher. They covered her with more blankets. Paul went in the ambulance with Maurine. She was taken to the Emergency Ward.

A doctor and several nurses attended to Maurine's injuries. X-rays had to be taken of Maurine's neck and left leg. The doctor had to set her neck and leg. Maurine would have to stay in the hospital for a period of time until she could use crutches to walk. She remained in the hospital for a month because of her broken neck. Her left leg was placed in a cast.

Maurine didn't like having to lie in bed helpless. She had been independent all her life. This was a real challenge for her. She would have to recover before she could be independent again. She finally went home after a month.

The doctor told Maurine she would need to have someone stay with her until she became more capable of walking and doing household chores and cooking again. A home care person was assigned to look after Maurine. Maurine was concerned about her health. She wanted to regain her strength.

Maurine began praying that she would recover. The food at the hospital was not very nutritious in comparison to the way Maurine was used to preparing food for herself. She wasn't as healthy as she once was because of the setback of breaking her neck and left leg plus eating food that wasn't as vital and nutritional.

Maurine wondered if she would ever recover from her accident. She tried to remain positive. Yet, she felt discouraged and worried about her condition. Finally her neck began to heal slowly. She wore a neck brace. Her left leg began to mend. It took longer than she thought it would.

Within six months Maurine finally began to regain some of her strength. She sat outside in a wheelchair to enjoy her garden. Weeds had grown and the garden needed to be watered. Maurine missed working in her garden. She missed her daily walks. She sat in the fresh air in the sunlight to restore herself.

In time Maurine regained most of her strength. Her neck and leg finally healed. Maurine began taking short walks. She began to water her garden again. She hoped in time to make a full recovery.

FORTY-EIGHT

VICTORIES

We experience victories in our lives when we are positive and make worthwhile decisions. Every thought, word and deed can help us accomplish specific victories. Victories are triumphant moments in our lives.

The victory of looking within to our higher self for truth and knowledge will help us develop interiorly. Inner truths awaken us to God reality and eternal knowledge. The victory of overcoming bad habits and way of the lower self is a real step in the right direction.

Every step to improve oneself is a victory on the path of spiritual attainment. Creative people experience victories in their creative endeavors. An artist may paint a variety of worthwhile paintings. His or her artwork may be displayed in art galleries and art museums. Many people may come to see the beautiful paintings.

A musician may perfect his or her technique in playing the piano. He or she may become a concert pianist. This person may play at concerts and impress many people so they will appreciate his or her piano performances. The pianist may feel victorious because he or she has perfected his or her skills in playing the piano.

A victorious person feels more elated and uplifted when he or she experiences success and happiness. Success comes from achieving worthwhile projects and research. A victorious person feels good about himself and others because of his achievements and accomplishments.

Victorious people are able to serve humanity. Their positive accomplishments help other people to be prosperous and successful. Every victory is of benefit to humanity. Defeats can be turned into victories. Each person can pursue happiness and success in order to experience victory.

FORTY-NINE

ATTENDING CHURCH

Going to a church is generally a healthy experience. People who go to church participate in prayers and sing religious songs. They listen to ministers, priests or special speakers.

Ministers speak about religious values and beliefs. A minister usually quotes from the Bible. The minister quotes about specific points of view and issues that the disciples of Jesus wrote and spoke about. Jesus' disciples wrote about Jesus' teachings. The disciples wrote Gospels which have been put in the New Testament of the Bible.

People who attend church tend to be more adjusted to life. They believe in Jesus' teachings. Jesus spoke about living by the Golden Rule. Jesus spoke about doing unto others as you would want to be treated. Give to others and serve others.

Churchgoers participate in church activities and programs. They put on church bazaars, church carnivals and church picnics. They have fun participating in these activities. Churchgoers have a sense of belonging when they attend church. They can make friends with other churchgoers.

Friendships with churchgoers can be spiritual relationships. Spiritual unity can occur between churchgoers. Ministers and priests encourage church members to become close with the love of Jesus Christ.

Christians claim to be saved by Jesus Christ. They say that Jesus Christ works in them. There are church weddings, potlucks and special events. Singles groups exist as well. Churchgoers have an opportunity to benefit by going to church.

FIFTY

DIARY TIME

Keeping a daily diary can help you express your daily experiences and feelings. Every experience of significance can be recorded. Day by day descriptions of what you experience can be written in your diary.

You can read and review your daily diary. You should write the date and time you are writing in your diary. State the experiences that you think are important to write in your diary.

Your diary will become a book about your most important experiences in your daily life. You should keep your diary in a safe place. Your diary is your private accounting of your life.

Anne Frank who lived in Amsterdam wrote her experiences in a personal diary during World War II. She wrote about how her family lived in the hidden, upper floor rooms of her father's office building. They had to keep quiet so no one would hear them in the street and betray them to the Nazis.

Anne Frank described how her family had to endure starvation. They had to share a small amount of food. They were hungry most of the time. They had to be silent during the day because people worked in the building. Anne spent time in a quiet corner writing in her diary in order to keep busy.

After two years and one month the Frank family was betrayed and found by the German Nazis. They were sent to concentration camps where almost all of them died, including Anne. Only her father survived and he eventually returned to Holland after the war.

Anne Frank's diary was found hidden in the upper floor where the Frank family hid from the German Nazis. Her diary became very famous because she described what experiences her family endured during World War II.

People visit the building where Anne Frank and her family stayed in hiding for just over two years. Tourists are able to see where Anne Frank and her family lived. Her diary has been produced into a film. She has become famous as a writer of a diary which revealed what life was life during World War II in Holland.

Diaries can be valuable if well written with details. Diaries can be used to describe important experiences, events and issues.

FIFTY-ONE

AMAZON WOMEN

Amazon women existed long ago in South America at the Amazon River. They dwelled in nearby jungles close to the Amazon River. Amazon women lived only with other women. Men were not allowed to live with Amazon women.

Amazon women were warriors. They were able to defend themselves against other people as well as wild animals. These women were very strong and capable of doing many things. They were excellent hunters and craftswomen.

Men were allowed to come into Amazon villages for very brief periods of time to mate with women in the Amazon village. Then the men were expected to leave. Otherwise, these men would be forced out of the Amazon village or be killed by Amazon women.

Amazon women were skillful in making bows and arrows to use for hunting. They gathered jungle fruit, vegetables and herbs. They were health conscious. They were also self reliant and intelligent.

Amazon women were attractive with long black hair, brown skin and eyes. They were physically fit. They could run swiftly and they could survive in the jungle. The Amazon women moved into a stone city.

The Inca Army of Peru tried to destroy the Amazon women near the Amazon River in Peru. However, the Amazon women won the battle because they were excellent warriors. Amazon women lived for many years and they prospered and thrived near the Amazon River. The Amazon, women village was the only civilization where only women existed and lived together in harmony without depending on men to protect them.

Amazon women made beautiful jewelry from gold. They prayed to gods of nature. They worshipped the Sun. Their sun god was ruler of the world according to the Amazon women. They were religious and had self discipline.

Girl babies were raised by the Amazon women. Boy babies were eliminated from the Amazon civilization. Girls grew up to maintain the civilization in the wilderness.

Amazon women may not have had a written language. They had a spoken language. They communicated intelligently. Amazon women had a stone calendar. They continued to survive because they had enough food and water. They were able to protect themselves from all dangers. They were able to endure heat and very warm weather.

All Amazon women were treated equally. They made intelligent decisions and became leaders in their Amazon civilization.

Fifty-Two

Marco Polo's Remarkable Experiences in Asia and the Middle East

Marco Polo was an explorer from Venice, Italy in the 13th Century. He traveled for twenty-four years through the East. Marco Polo wrote a book entitled The Travels of Marco Polo, which became an inspirational book for explorers to read.

Marco Polo began his book The Travels of Marco Polo this way. "Ye Emperors, Kings, Dukes, Marquises, Earls and Knights and all other people desirous of knowing the diversities of the races of mankind as well as the diversities of kingdoms, provinces and regions of all parts of the East. Read this book and ye will find in it the greatest and most marvelous characteristics of the peoples especially in China, Armenia, Persia, India and Tartary."

As Marco Polo spoke the above dialogue, Rustichello, a cellmate companion in a Venetian prison wrote down every word. Marco Polo told the story of his twenty-four year journey through the East.

Marco Polo was the son of a wealthy, Italian merchant. So Marco

Polo became a wealthy merchant as well. While Marco Polo spent a year in prison in Venice after he returned from his worldly travels he wrote his descriptive book about his travels.

Rustichello said to Marco after each story, "No man has ever before seen such wonders!" Marco answered, "But who would believe me? If I recorded the truth I would only be branded a liar!" But Rustichello would press his friend. "The truth in the end must win out over falsehood," he told Marco.

Marco Polo recorded information about his travels along the Silk Road known as the network of roads and trails that linked Europe with the East. Marco wrote about his experiences in the court of the great Kublai Khan. Rustichello wrote to Marco Polo's father asking him to send to the prison in Genoa the notes of Marco Polo about his travels in the East.

Weeks later a guard unlocked Marco's cell door and he handed Marco Polo a package which contained his precious notes. Marco used parchment paper made from animal skins. He wrote with goose feather pens. Rustichello wrote Marco Polo's story down.

Marco Polo continued to write about his Eastern travels and adventures. Marco was born in 1254 to Niccolo Polo. Niccolo and his brother Maffeo Polo left on a trading mission to the city of Constantinople. They were gone for six years so Marco wasn't able to know his father and uncle.

In 1260 a new emperor had taken power in Cathay, another word for China. His name was Kublai Khan. He was the grandson of the "fierce" Mongol warrior Genghis Khan, whose armies had conquered a vast area of Asia. Genghis Khan's empire included modern-day Mongolia, China, Russia and Iran. His Mongol warriors may have conquered places in Europe if Genghis had not died suddenly in 1227.

Kublai Khan, the next Mongol emperor, remained as powerful and rich as it had been when his grandfather ruled. Kublai Khan wanted his empire to be at peace. His merchants could trade with the nations of Western Europe.

The Polo brothers were eager to take part in trade with Cathay, known as China. "They took a cargo of gems eastward, riding on horseback into Mongol lands." Eventually, the Polos met emissaries from Kublai Khan. Kublai Khan was willing to meet Europeans.

The Polos made a trip to the city of Shandu where Kublai Khan kept a summer palace. Shandu is called Beijing today in China. Beijing is the capital city. Kublai Khan showed great hospitality to Niccolo and Maffeo. They stayed in Shandu for nearly nine years.

The Polos eventually returned to Venice fifteen years later. Noccolo Polo found that his wife had died and that his son Marco was a teenager. Young Marco, who was seventeen years old was anxious to join his father and uncle in their adventures.

Niccolo Polo felt his son Marco was ready to travel with him. The Polos met with the new Pope Gregory X. They gave a letter from Kublai Khan. After the new Pope read the Khan's letter he sent for 100 Christian clergymen to go with the Polos to Cathay. Only two friars joined the Polo caravan.

The Polos took the Silk Road to Cathay (China). The Silk Road was the name given to several routes that linked Europe and the Far East. Along the Silk Road the Polos experienced trading for silk, a soft and elegant fabric created from the cocoons of mulberry silk worms. They gathered gold, ivory from exotic animals, plants, spices, etc.

From Java, merchants carried nutmeg; from India, ginger and cinnamon. From Tibet traders would deal in musk. Jewels were also carried back and forth, diamonds from Aolconda, rubies from Badakhsan, turquoise from Yedz, pearls from Ceylon. From Cathay merchants would trade porcelain.

The silk people were known as the Chinese, who helped create myths about the fabrics in order to preserve their monopoly on its trade. Chinese rulers established inspection stations along the Silk Road to make sure no one smuggled out their secrets to weaving silk.

The Polos were not like other merchants. They intended to travel virtually the entire length of the Silk Road. With so many valuable goods making their ways east and west, bandits were drawn to the Silk Road.

The slow-moving caravans were easy targets for a few armed men with swift horses. Danger lurked around the curves of every mountain, in every desert oasis, along the banks of every river. Merchants were forced to hire armed guards to protect their caravans. Eventually, walls and forts were built along the Silk Road to add further protection for the merchants. It is believed that sections of the Great Wall of China were built to protect Silk Road merchants from bandits.

Very few merchants traveled the full length of the road. They covered part of the journey selling their goods close to home and then returning with their profits. Other merchants would then resell the goods to other merchants and so on.

Marco, Maffeo and Niccolo crossed deserts, including the vast and scorching Gobi in Mongolia. In Central Asia they would climb tall mountains and march through deep snow. They traveled by horse, camel and yak. They sailed up rivers aboard oar-powered galleys. They even walked part of the way.

The Polos were often delayed by heavy rains that turned the road into mud. In the deserts, strong winds would cause blinding sandstorms. Avalanches occurred in the mountains. Roads were closed. The Polos had to find paths around the tons of rocks. They had to be on the lookout for bandits.

Marco Polo saw Mount Ararat where Noah's Ark came to rest after the Great Flood that is reported in the Bible. Marco was more interested in the terrain around the mountain than in its biblical significance. He noted that Mount Ararat's lower slopes had plenty of water and provided for excellent grazing for cattle and sheep, in Georgia, a mountainous region near Russia.

Marco noticed the area was rich in oil. "It is a substance spurting from the ground and used for burning in lamps," he wrote. Marco Polo found "a remarkable material which can be spun into thread and woven into cloths that will not burn when thrust into the fire." The material was asbestos.

Marco Polo tasted coconut on the journey. "It is a nut the size of a man's head, pleasant to taste and white as milk." On seeing his first crocodile, Marco described it as a "huge serpent, ten paced in length, with jaws wide enough to swallow a man."

Marco Polo wrote about a port city, Hormuz where the Polo caravan went. "Merchants came her by ship from India," Marco wrote, "bringing all sorts of spices and precious stones and pearls and cloths of silk, gold, elephants' tusks and many other wares."

Marco observed that the people of Hormuz lived on salted fish, onions and a fruit from a palm tree called dates. He said the natives refused to eat our wheaten bread and meat because they thought it would make them sick.

The Polos continued their journey by food because they knew ships were not safe. Marco wrote, "Their ships are very bad. They are not fastened with iron nails but stitched together with a thread made of coconut husks."

The Polos went north to Persia. They met up with Karuanas, a half-Indian, half-Mongol people in the Persian desert. Marco wrote that the Karuanas were said to have mastered "magical and diabolical arts by means of which they were enabled to produce darkness, obscuring the light of day to such a degree that persons were invisible to one another."

The Polos were attacked by the Karuana raiding party. Some of the Polo caravan were captured and some of them were killed by these raiders. The Polos hid in a nearby tower. They eventually escaped.

Two monks in the caravan were lost. The friars became nervous. So they returned to Italy to avoid bandit attacks. After leaving Persia the Polo caravan entered Badakhshan, a cold, mountainous region which is called Afghanistan today.

Marco believed the Muslim people in Afghanistan descended from Alexander the Greek. He was a Greek conqueror who explored Asia and the Middle East around 330 B.C. Marco observed the people of Badakhshan were masters of horsemanship. He wrote his suspicion that their strong and swift horses were descended from one of Alexander's war horses.

Unfortunately, Marco became ill in Badakhshan. So the Polos were delayed for a year in order for Marco to recover. When Marco was strong enough the caravan continued through the Pamir Mountains.

Today, the sheep of the Pamir Mountains are named after Marco Polo. In Latin, the Pamir sheep are known as Ovis Poli. Ovis is the Latin word for sheep.

Marco wrote, "No birds fly here because of the height and the cold. And I assure you that because of this great cold, fire is not bright and fire changes color. It does not burn well. Food does not cook well." The Polos fire lacked the oxygen in the air. So the Polos' cooking fire lacked the fuel they needed to burn.

It took fifty-two days to cross the Pamir Mountains. The Polos came to a great plain in Western China. The Polos stopped in Kahsgar, Yarkland and Khotan. Kashgan produced cotton cloth. Yarkland had expert craftsmen. Khotan had many farms, vineyards and gardens.

From Khatan the Polos faced another "stretch of rough travel" before they reached the palace of Kublai Khan. This was the Gobi Desert, in the Gobi Desert the Polos walked to one oasis to another one. Daylight temperatures soared to 100 degrees Fahrenheit and there were terrible sandstorms. At night the temperature dropped to a low temperature. So the Polo caravan were cold even under their blankets at their campfires.

For years the Chinese called the Gobi the 'Flowing Sands' because the fierce Gobi wind constantly rearranged the positions of the desert's sand dunes. The Polos could hear the sounds of trhe shifting sands. "Do not stray from your caravan," the Polos were told by an experienced desert traveler while they rested at an oasis. "Voices may lead you in the wrong direction and cause you to be hopelessly lost."

The Polos trudged on across the Gobi Desert. It took them thirty days to cross the Gobi Desert. They arrived in Shandu and they were met by an emperor's escort. They were led to see and meet the Kublai Khan.

It was 1275. The Polos had been on their journey for nearly four years. They had endured the hardships of the deserts, the mountains and the jungles. They had escaped from bandits and overcome sickness. Their journey was 12,000 miles. They would finally meet Kublai Khan.

Marco, his father and uncle were led to the palace of Kublai Khan. They bowed to show respect for the great leader. The Khan ordered them to stand and he expressed his great joy at seeing the brothers again. The Khan asked who Marco was. Niccolo replied, "Your majesty, this is my son and your servant." The great Khan replied, "He is welcome and it pleases me much."

The Polos took the opportunity to look around the Khan's spectacular palace. The palace was located inside a fortified inner city within Shandu. The walls of the palace were decorated with carved dragons and painting of birds, animals and war scenes. The roof shone in the sunshine with its spectrum of colors: yellow, red, blue, green and violet.

The Khan had beautiful trees from around the world planted not far from the palace. The Khan loved trees. He had rare specimens planted there. On top of the hill called Green Mount there was a magnificent pavilion where the emperor would worship. The Polos came to a big lake with a variety of fish for the Khan to eat.

Kublai Khan had four wives who lived in the palace. Ten thousand guards watched over the palace. Behind the Green Mount were the Khan's stables with stalls for his 1,000 white horses. The Khan's oldest son, Chinkin, lived in a smaller palace near Kublai Khan. Chinkin would become ruler of the Mongol empire. Kublai Khan had twenty-one other sons and four wives.

Kublai Khan had banquets in large halls near the palace. His servants served enough food for 6,000 people. The emperor sat on an elevated pedestal. When the banquet was finished entertainers and dancers would amuse the guests until dawn.

Every year on September 28th, the emperor's birthday, 20,000 noblemen arrived at the palace all wearing golden robes decorated with jewels and pearls of enormous value. Another large celebration was held on the New Year when Kublai Khan was presented with gifts of gold, silver, precious stones and beautiful horses. 5,000 elephants would parade in Shandu. After the parade the noblemen would gather in a great hall. Everyone bowed down until their foreheads touched the floor. Then they ate food and had drinks.

The Kahn was shown great respect. People in his company had to lower their voices and behave humbly. Visitors had to take off their shoes before going into the palace.

Marco observed how bath water was heated. The Khan's servants used a large quantity of fuel in the form of "black stones." Marco became familiar with heated coal.

Shandu was a large, populated city. Roads lead from Shandu to all corners of Cathay (China). The Khan employed messengers on horseback who could bring him news from distant parts of his huge empire in a few days. The Khan had also set up a post office run by messengers. More than 10,000 people lived in Shandu. Messengers carried small packages on horseback from place to place along a system of roads.

Marco Polo found that Kublai Khan wanted his subjects to live a decent life. If storms or swarms of insects ruined their harvests he gave them food. They didn't have to pay taxes. If a family was hit by a disaster the family members were given food and clothes anyway.

Children without a family were brought up in special institutions. Many hospitals were built for the people. The Khan had an interest in seeing that his people were well taken care of. He knew it was best to help the needy, knowing that one day they would be ready to return the favor by becoming hard workers.

One of Kublai Khan's great accomplishments was building a Great Canal. This waterway stretched 1,000 miles from Shandu to Hangehou. The canal made it much easier to travel from the capital to the southern part of China.

The emperor encouraged education and learning. He established schools and promoted the study of astronomy and geography. Kublai Khan has trees planted along both sides of every big road. Kublai Khan was also interested in religion. He was shown the Bible that the Polos brought to China. He observed the holidays of four major religious groups. They were Christians, Muslims, Jews and Buddhists.

"I respect and honor all four great prophets, Jesus Christ, Mohammed, Moses and Buddha, so that I can appeal to any one of them in heaven," explained Kublai Khan.

Marco Polo became well acquainted with Kublai Khan. Marco visited Burma, Korea, Tibet and India. After living in the Molgol Empire for approximately twenty years the Polos returned to Venice in 1295.

The Polos asked the Khan if they could leave China. The Khan was seventy-six. He didn't want them to leave. However, he allowed them to go. He gave them thirteen ships. They sailed off through the Yellow Sea through a strait that separates Taiwan from the mainland of China. The Polos journeyed across the China Sea through the Bay of Bengal and the Indian Ocean to the Arabian Sea and Persian Gulf. The Polos stayed in Persia nine months. When they heard that Kublai Kahn had died the Polos decided to go back to Venice. Kublai's son and successor, Chinkin Khan stopped peaceful trade between the East and West. The Polos traveled to Constantinople named after King Constantine. This city was unique with magnificent architecture and an interesting culture.

Once the Polos returned to Venice in Italy they were amazed at how life had changed. The Polos had been gone twenty-four years. Marco Polo was forty-one years old. He was a middle-aged man. The trip home had been difficult and the three men were dressed in rags.

The Polos had sewn rubies, diamonds and emeralds into their clothes so they would not be stolen on the journey. The family staged a lavish banquet to welcome home the Polos. Marco spoke about the wonders he had seen.

Marco Polo's book, <u>A Description of the World</u> was the first best seller. It was very popular and the story was translated into many languages. For over 700 years people have enjoyed reading <u>The Book of Marco Polo</u>.

Marco Polo lived to be seventy years old. He was a great explorer. Marco was an adventurer, scholar and diplomat in the 13th Century. He informed others of his rare and unusual experiences in Asia and the Middle East. He encouraged trade between the East and the West. His experiences in Asia and the Middle East helped Europeans realize more about life in Asia and the Middle East.

FIFTY-THREE

ANCIENT CITIES IN THE WORLD

Ancient cities exist around the world. Many of them are in ruins. Ancient Rome still stands near modern Rome. It has sunk much lower than modern Rome. There are remnants of Roman, stone buildings. Columns still exist at proof of ancient Rome.

The Roman Coliseum still exists in Rome. It was built by a Roman emperor over 2,500 B.C. years ago. Stones were removed from the Coliseum to build other buildings. Roman gladiators performed in the Coliseum.

Ancient Rome is recognized because Romans were rulers of the world for over a thousand years. Their architecture was unique. They built homes and public buildings with stones, thick clay and clay baked tile.

Roman baths took place in large, Roman pools. Romans bathed and went swimming. The climate was hot and humid in Rome. Bathing was a frequent activity. Water cooled Romans. They kept clean by bathing.

Baghdad is an ancient city in Iraq. Iraq was in Persia during ancient times. Baghdad has many gardens with desert plants. Palm trees exist here. Ancient Persian temples and palaces existed in Baghdad.

Persian temples were designed with spectacular, mosaic, stone walls and floors. Turquoise and blue, mosaic, stones were put together in intricate patterns. Persian temples were built with arches and round topped doorways. The prayer room in the temples had no furniture. Moslems sat on the mosaic-tile floors to worship Allah. They often kneeled and bowed their heads to the floor while they prayed.

Persian temples had high ceilings in Baghdad. These temples look magnificent. Temples in Iraq still are beautiful. Bombing in 2003 has destroyed some palaces. These palaces were occupied by Saddam Hussein and his followers.

Athens, Patras and Ithaca are ancient cities in Greece. Athens was the cradle of Western civilization. Corinthian, ornate columns exist on Greek temples in Athens. The Parthenon is an ancient Greek temple in Athens. Greek treasures were stored in the Parthenon. An enormous stone statue of Zeus stands in the center of the Parthenon. This temple is located on a hill above the city of Athens today. The Acropolis is an ancient temple in Athens on a hill as well.

There are ruins of other Greek temples and homes in Athens, Patras and Ithaca in Greece. Remnants of Greek columns exist in these three, Greek cities from ancient times. Greek temples still exist throughout Greece in different cities. These ancient temples were in ancient cities known as Delos, Florina and Sparta.

Arenas for sports were once used by Greek gladiators and warriors to perform for Greek audiences. Plumbing and water was conducted in pipes in some of these ancient cities.

We should appreciate ruins from ancient cities because we should learn all we can about ancient cultures and civilizations. Ancient architecture was massive and grand. Stone buildings were built with heavy stones. Majestic columns are a thing of the past. Ancient columns were tremendous and strong. Many columns have endured extreme climates. We can learn how to build by using ancient, architectural plans.

Constantinople is an ancient city in the Middle East. It is called Istanbul today. Constantine, the first Christian emperor lived in Constantinople. The largest temple in Constantinople, known as Sophia is an ancient, enormous temple. This grand building stands out as the grandest temple in the Middle East.

Christians build Sophia around 1,600 years ago. They decorated this enormous temple with Christian paintings and statues. Eventually Moslems took over Sophia after winning a battle with the Christians. Sophia has become a Moslem temple. Moslem artwork has replace Christian art inside Sophia. This temple is a landmark representing an ancient reminder of majestic architecture.

Fifty-Four

How to Use a Dictionary

Dictionaries were created many years ago. As languages were created and words were written down scholars wrote definitions for each word recorded. Then words were organized alphabetically by ABC and on.

Daniel Webster created a dictionary in English several hundred years ago. He wrote more than one definition for each word. Some words sounded like another word. However, these words had different meanings. Some words are spelled exactly a certain way. Yet these words have different meanings.

Each word in a dictionary has phonetic sounds and marking to help people sound out each word correctly. A person can learn to sound out words phonetically by using a dictionary.

Each word in the dictionary is a part of speech. The part or parts of speech are abbreviated before the definitions. The part of speech describes how words are used in sentences.

A glossary is put in dictionaries in the back. Certain words are listed which can be described more thoroughly. There are regional dialects in the United States of America. A map is illustrated at the beginning of Webster's New World Dictionary.

Foreign sounds are listed. Symbols are listed. Key words are given for each symbol. These pronunciation symbols are: a I oo oi ou u ur a ar b d f h h j k l m n p r s t v w y z ch sh th zh. There are also and a with an accent mark over it, an a with a double accent mark, an I with a line over it, a double o with a line over it, and yoo with a line over the two o's.

There is a guild for the use of the Webster's Dictionary. "The main entry work is arranged. All main entries include single words, hyphenated and unhyphenated compounds, proper names, prefixes, suffixes and abbreviations which are listed in strict alphabetical order and are set in large, boldface type."

Example:

"black (blak) adj.

Black (blak) Hugo (LaFayette)

Black alder

Black-and-blue (-anbloo) adj.

Black.berry (ber'e) n.

Bldg.

-ble(b;l)…"

"Note that in the biographical entry only the last or family name, that part preceding the comma, has been considered in alphabetization. When two or more persons with the same family name are entered, they are dealt with in a single entry block, arranged in alphabetical order by first name. Biographical and geographical names that are identical in form are kept in separate blocks."

"Inflected forms regarded as irregular or offering difficulty in spelling are entered in small boldface immediately following the part-of-speech labels. They are truncated where possible and syllabified and pronounced where necessary."

"Plurals formed regularly by adding –s to the singular (or –es after s, x, z, ch and sh), as bats, boxes, are not normally indicated. Plurals are shown when formed irregularly as for nouns with a –y ending that changes to –ies and for those having variant forms, those having different forms for different meanings, compound nouns, etc."

Example:

"cit.y… n, pl. cit'ies.

Bole-ro… n, pl, -ros

tooth… n, pl, teeth (teth)

a-moe-ba… n, pl –bas, -bae (-be)

die… n, pl. for 1 & 2, dice (dis)

  for 3 & 4, dies (diz)

son-in-law… n, pl sons'-in-law'…"

"If an irregular plural is so altered in spelling that it would appear at some distance from the singular form, it is entered additionally in its proper alphabetical place. Verb forms regarded as regular and not normally indicated include: (a) present tenses formed by adding s to the infinitive (or –es after s, x, z, ch and sh) as waits, searches; (b) past tenses and past participles formed by simply adding –ed to the infinitive with no other changed I the verb form, such as waiting, searching."

"Principal parts are give for irregular verbs including those in which the final e is dropped in forming the present participle, those which always or optionally repeat the final consonant in all principal parts, those in which –y changes to –ie– in the past tenst and the past participle, and the second is the form for the present participle."

Example:

"make…vt, made, making…

Sip… vt, vi, sipped, sipping…"

"Where three forms are given, separated from one another by commas, the first represents the past tense, the second the past participle, and the third the present participle."

Example:

"swim… vi, swam, swum, swimming"

"If a principal part of a verb is so altered in spelling that it would appear at some distance from the infinitive form, it is entered additionally in its proper alphabetical place."

Example:

"said… pt. & pp. of say"

When the name of an animal or plant is entered in this dictionary, its scientific name is included parenthetically in the definition. All animals and plants have been given modern Latin or Latinized names by biologists in accordance with rules prescribed by international codes of zoological and botanical nomenclature and have been systematically classified into certain categories or taxa, that discriminate among organisms."

Language changes from generation to generation. Slang language has been added to dictionaries. Words from dialects may be added to dictionaries. Word meanings must be accurate and clear. Enough language should be written in the dictionary. There are over 100,000 words in a complete dictionary.

Grammar must be properly used in dictionaries. There should not be any contradictions in the use of words. All languages include patterns of sound. The study of the origin and development of words, their forms and meanings in seeking the "etymon," the true sense of words.

FIFTY-FIVE

THE PLEIADIANS

The Pleiades is a constellation which is trillions of miles away from out solar system. There are nine, major, star systems. There are actually 250 stars which humanity cannot see with the naked eye in the Pleiades.

Nine major stars exist in the Pleiades. The are Atlas, Pleione, Alcyone, Merope, Electra, Maia, Celaeno, Taygeta and Asterope. Only six stars are visible to our naked eyes.

On December 21, 2012 our Earth will line up with Alcyone on the galactic equator. This happens every 26,000 years which is one galactic year. This is the end of one galactic year. The Mayans say the Pleiadian gods will return to Earth on December 21, 2012.

Erra is a planet in the star system of Taygeta. Pleiadians from Erra have traveled to Earth millions of years ago. They were tall, slender, blond haired, human-like beings who were peaceful and enlightened.

Pleiadians could communicate telepathically. They communicated about their way of life. They understood how to produce pure energy. They ate fruit and drank nutritional, fruit drinks. These Pleiadians awakened ancient Lumurians and Atlanteans.

Pleiadians travel in spaceships faster than the speed of light because they use a pure energy without sound. They have traveled to Earth frequently through the years. The Hawaiians and Balenese peoples have been enlightened by Pleiadians.

Pleiadians understand the laws of the Cosmos. They live by the laws of love, unity, centralization, karma (cause and effect), and other laws. The reality of magnetism, gravity and polarities are more laws the Pleiadians understand.

Erra is a planet with good climate in the solar system of Taygeta in the Pleiades. The sky is a violet-blue. The climate is mild. The Pleiadians, who have lived on Erra for millions of years, live in peace and harmony. Their central government promotes justice, worthwhile endeavors and goodwill towards all Pleiadians.

The Pleiadians still contact certain people on Earth to encourage Earthlings to live in peace and harmony. They encourage us to stop wars. We should learn to live by the laws of love, unity and brotherhood.

The Pleiadians are commonly believed to originate from another universe. Their ancestry can be traced to a planetary race called Lyrans, whose progress in space travel outpaced their spiritual growth. The Lyrans split up into two groups. One group focused on technology. The other group emphasized spirituality. The latter group left their planet know known as Lyra and settled on Earth.

On Earth the race of Lyrans from the Pleiades developed further as another group. They pursued peace. Then these beings left Earth and settled in the Pleiades. Humans are sometimes seen as ancestors of the Pleiadians.

The Pleiadians also began to reconnect with Earth, their former home and took on the task of helping this civilization evolve towards spiritual maturity. It is said that there are a number of Pleiadians who have incarnated on Earth in order to awaken dormant energies within the human race.

The Pleiadians are described as Caucasians with light hair coloring and light blue or brown eyes. They range from five to seven feet tall. Pleiadians are sometimes referred to as Nordics because they are similar in appearance to northern, European races.

Often described as extraordinary dimensional travelers, the Pleiadians are said to facilitate movement and communication between dimensional planes. They are very aware of travel through time and space. They guard the gates of transformation between dimensions.

Many people believe that the Pleiadians have been in contact with the Earth for many eons. Between Huelo and Hana is the small village of Wailua, where a man and his wife reported flying disk landings and actual contact with physical beings from another world.

In 1987 Leilani Brissette Dearing, a Ph.D. with a professional projection, reported alien beings with basically human appearance and height, emerged from the spacecraft that landed in their backyard. These beings had light golden skin and their eyes were black. The aliens took her aboard their spacecraft. They claimed to be from the Pleiades.

Ancient Hawaiians contain literature about Pleiadians in Hawaii. A secret, underwater, Pleiadian, space agent who was in contact with the United Nations, told Steve Omar that he witnessed a UFO emerging from former, military, intelligence agents.

Contacts with Pleiadians are detailed in ancient writings fro India, Tibet, Manchuria, Sumeria, Egypt, Babylonia, Maya-Meso America, Chaldea and other regions. They gave instructions in agriculture, textiles, architecture and other building blocks of early civilization.

We can learn from the Pleiadians how to promote and maintain peace and well being. The future of our planet depends on how we live and learn how to relate well with one another.

Fifty-Six

Fossils

Fossils are ancient animal and plant imprints in rocks and stones. There are many fossils embedded deep in layers of rocks and sediment. Fossils are dug up by paleontologists and botanists. They study fossils in order to determine what ancient animals and plants existed millions of years ago.

Fossils with ancient fish are imprinted even at the Grand Canyon. This proves that the Grand Canyon was under the ocean long ago. The Earth has changed a lot in millions of years.

At one time many, massive continents were joined together. Wild animals roamed these enormous continents. Then the continents began to sink. Cataclysms occurred and land animals suddenly died. Their bodies were crashed into rocks forming fossils.

Many fossils help paleontologists in determining the different time periods that exist. Fossils collected can be studied to find out when, where and how life has changed in millenniums of time. Time cycles have occurred and have been recorded by archaeologists and paleontologists.

Fossils are tangible proof of ancient imprints of animals and plants that existed long ago. These fossils are historical markings which are used to expose life on Earth.

Human bones have been stored in rocks and deep sediments. Human bones have been found which existed a million years ago. Human bones exist in some fossils. These bones are proof of human life on Earth. Ancient bones were found in Africa of an African woman who lived at least one million years ago. These ancient bones are used as evidence of human existence on Earth.

Fossils are valuable because they are physical objects which show that animals and plants lived on Earth in specific locations in ancient times.

FIFTY-SEVEN

SPIRITUAL PREDICTIONS

Spiritual revelations and predictions have been revealed throughout time. The Bible is a testament of different revelations. In the Old Testament Abraham stated revelations. Daniel, who was a prophet, made predictions about the future of his people.

Moses revealed revelations. He brought forth the Ten Commandments. Lot was given revelations by angels about Sodom and Gomorrah being destroyed. Lot and his family were told to leave Sodom. He walked away from Sodom with his wife and two daughters. He was told not to look back. Lot's wife was tempted. She turned and looked back. She was covered with debris.

Noah was contacted and told to build an Ark. He took two of each kind of animal with him in the Ark. His wife and seven children and servants boarded the Ark along with the animals. When they all were aboard the Ark it began to rain heavily. It began to flood as predicted. Noah and his family were the only humans to survive the disastrous flood.

Noah and his family ended up in Turkey. Their Ark has been found in the mountains in Turkey on Mount Ararat. Noah and his family began a new civilization in Turkey. The revelation came true.

In the New Testament more revelations were stated. In Genesis it was predicted that Messiah would be born to establish a new kingdom. Three wise men, who were Kings in the Middle East, saw the Bethlehem star. They followed this bright object in the sky. This star could have been a comet with a tail.

The three wise men knew about the prediction or revelation that a great Messiah would be born. They followed the Bethlehem Star until they found the stable where Jesus Christ was born. They brought gifts to give to Jesus Christ.

FIFTY-EIGHT

VISUAL APPARITIONS

Visual apparitions exist. We have an astral eye in which we are able to see psychic visions. We have visual apparitions when we dream.

Some people have psychic abilities which are more developed. These people are able to duplicate astral images of people. The astral images look like real people. However, they are astral forms which disappear.

I have seen many astral images of people whose astral presence makes itself visible to my astral eyes. These astral images appear in front of me. Some of them stare at me. Other astral images are not staring at me. Some astral images are pleasant. Other astral images are startling and unpleasant.

I do not expect an astral image to appear before me. I may be sitting in my recliner chair resting. When I open my eyes there is an image right before me. Quite often I am quite startled. I don't expect a visual image of someone to be standing before me. These images last for seconds. Then they disappear.

I have seen astral images of my deceased parents, my two deceased brothers and my sister who is still living. They appeared very much like they looked on Earth. My mother appeared younger however. My eldest brother looked nearly the same as he did on Earth. My other brother looked lighter than he did on Earth.

I didn't expect to see the astral images of my deceased parents and brothers. They appeared before me unexpectedly at different times. There may be a reason for us to see visual apparitions. Our loved ones who are deceased may want to see us again. They want us to know they are alright on the other side.

FIFTY-NINE

SOYA PRODUCTS

There are a variety of soya products at health stores and even at nutritional centers and in some regular, grocery stores. Loma Linda products have been produced for years by The Seventh Day Adventists.

There are soya patties, soya wieners, soya burgers and smooth soya loaf you can purchase in cans. Most soya products are bought in cans. Soya bean powder can be used in soya shakes and also sprinkled on cereal.

Some soya products are put into casseroles. These casserole dishes may be produced into frozen foods. Some soya foods can be dried and put into plastic sacks. Soya beans can be used in different ways.

Soya products can be preserved easily because they are not meat products. Soya products are high in protein and amino acids. Soya products have quite a lot more protein than meat. Soya products are grown in the ground. Soya beans are a natural food.

Vegetarians eat soya products. They may eat some dairy products such as milk, eggs and cheese. Vegetarians can drink soya milk. Soya milk is delicious in cereal. Use stevia in place of sugar.

Soya beans are grown by many farmers who want soya beans to be purchased and used by many people. Soya beans are worth growing. More and more people should eat soya products. They would be healthier if they were vegetarians.

SIXTY

LIVING IN A REST HOME

Living in a rest home is necessary for elderly people who are in need of more personal care. Three meals are provided every day. Each elderly resident is assigned a room. They may share a room with one or two people.

Some elderly people bring their own television and radio to the rest home for recreation. There are usually other activities such as card games, Scrabble, Checkers and other games played in the recreation room.

Elderly people go out into the garden to sit in the sun. They enjoy the sunshine and beauty of the gardens.

Each room must be cleaned regularly. Bedding such as sheets, pillowcases and mattress covers are changed as well. The rooms are swept and mopped regularly. The rooms are dusted and straightened out. Clothes and other personal items are stored in closets and drawers.

Some elderly people are more independent. Other older people are very dependent on the help of other people. Elderly people are capable of putting their belongings away in their closets and drawers.

It takes a while to adjust to a rest home. Newcomers must try to accept others around them. Getting along with other is important. Gossip should be avoided. Gossip can be very harmful and annoying.

Dinner parties and birthday celebrations are special occasions. Church choirs come to entertain elderly people. They sing choir music and holiday music.

Life in rest homes can be worthwhile especially for elderly people who have been isolated and shut in. They can cultivate new friendships. However, many elderly people do not like to leave their homes. They have lived for many years in their own homes. They must learn to accept their new lifestyle in a rest home.

SixtY-One

Vaudeville Entertainment

Vaudeville entertainment was very popular in the 18th and 19th Centuries. Women dressed in colorful, long dresses and open leg outfits with long, silk stockings. Men dressed in striped suits and top hats.

Vaudeville musicals were presented with singing and dancing. Dance routines were magnificent and very entertaining. Vaudeville entertainment was performed on stages. People came to the town and city stage door theaters to se vaudeville productions.

Melodramas were performed many years ago. Audiences participated by booing and hurrahing during dramatic scenes. There were heroes and villains in melodramas. This was the form of entertainment in the 17th and 18th Centuries.

It took talent to perform in vaudeville dramas and even in melodramas. Audiences sat on wooden benches or chairs. The curtain was drawn until the program began. A piano was played at the side of the stage near the audience.

The Ziegfeld Follies were a form of sophisticated, vaudeville entertainment. Women dressed in elaborate costumes. Men dressed in black suits and bow ties. Women wore fancy hairdos with long curls and fancy hats. They wore fancy shoes and stockings.

Audiences were highly entertained especially in New York City in the Broadway section of the city. The curtain rose and beautiful music was sung. Dance routines were spectacular. The Ziegfeld Follies was very successful and popular for many years.

Sixty-Two

Mystical Geometric Symbols

Mystical, geometric symbols exist. The Jews created a five pointed star which was symbolical. A six pointed star in another mystical symbol. These pointed stars were sacred symbols. They were esoteric for thousands of years.

Circles are mystical symbols. The center of a circle is a point of centralization. Every line around a circle is equidistant from the center point. Circles exist in nature. Designs of the Central Sun are circular. Circles are carved into sacred stones.

Triangular shapes represent the shape of pyramids. The pyramids in Egypt are sacred monuments built to worship Egyptian gods and pharaohs. Many pyramids were built for burial chambers for pharaohs of Egypt.

A cross is a mystical, sacred symbol in Christianity. A cross represents a symbol of crucifixion. Jesus Christ was sacrificed on a wooden cross. Christians wear a cross around their necks as a sacred symbol of Christianity.

A yin-yang symbol is a Chinese symbol of infinity. It represents a sacred eternity. The third eye symbol is another mystical symbol. This symbol is on an American dollar bill. It is called the Eye of Horus.

Hieroglyphs are sacred symbols used by Egyptians. Many hieroglyphs are carved on walls inside Egyptian temples and pyramids. These sacred symbols describe the religious beliefs and way of life of the Egyptians.

In Metaphysics a cross and key in a circle is a sacred symbol for Theosophy. This sacred symbol represents the key that unlocks the truth. The cross represents the holy symbol of Christ. The circle encompasses the key and cross. This metaphysical symbol is seen in Theosophical books and in a picture on the wall in The Temple of the People in Halcyon, California.

Sixty-Three

ANASTASIA FROM THE SIBERIAN TAIGA

Anastasia is a young woman who lives in a deserted bank of the Siberian Ob River which is thousands of kilometers from our so-called civilization. She was wearing an old jacket, long skirt and rubber galoshes. She was wrapped up in a shawl. Only her eyes were visible.

"Anastasia is indeed the most unusual phenomenon of our time," said Regina Jenson, Ph.D. "Anastasia possesses some mysterious abilities and knowledge of the primogenitors. She considers the basic science to be the science of imagery knowledge that was partially possessed by the priests of ancient Egypt."

The curing of many diseases are more of Anastasia's abilities. "As shown by later events, Anastasia is able to design the future and following her thoughts, this future begins to materialize in the real circumstances of our lives," she said.

Anastasia was "an uncommonly beautiful woman, about twenty-three with long, golden hair. The features of her face were regular. Her well tended skin was not weather beaten like other dwellers of the Siberian backwoods. She has large, kind, gray-blue eyes and lips. An unusual energy emanated from Anastasia's body which could be felt even at a distance," said Vladimir Megre.

Anastasia said, "When the inner, spiritual world of a person changes, new knowledge and abilities will be opened to him or her. A person may create wonderful worlds analogous to our Earthly world on other planets."

"Some kind of great power must have been concealed in the spiritual impulses of Anastasia, and this power seemingly overcomes the darkness that has conquered the world," Vladimir Megre said.

Anastasia said, "How a person can, in perfecting his or her living environment, protect the Earth even from meteorites and make the universe a more comfortable place in which to live is the solution to life on Earth."

Anastasia continues to live in Siberia in the woodlands. She lives a simple life of service. She has positive thoughts. She enlightens people she come in contact with. She lives a pure life in a remote place by herself. She is close to nature and God.